The Worry
Control
Workbook

Mary Ellen Copeland, M.S., M.A.

BARNES
&NOBLE
BOOKS
NEW YORK

This book is dedicated to Edward Mary Rose Anthes, whose assistance, love, and support carried me through the busy days and sleepless nights as this book was coming to fruition; to Martha Bauman, Allen Blair, and Teta Hilsdon, whose technical skills, knowledge, and expertise made this book happen; and to the many volunteers who participated in the focus groups, responded to questions in the extensive survey, and spent hours discussing with me their views and experiences.

An Irishman's Philosophy

There are only two things to worry about.
Either you are well or you are sick.
If you are well, then there is nothing to worry about.
But if you are sick, there are two things to worry about.
Either you will get well or you will die.
If you get well, then there is nothing to worry about.
If you die, there are only two things to worry about.
Either you will go to heaven or hell.
If you go to heaven, there is nothing to worry about.
But if you go to hell, you'll be so damn busy shaking
hands with friends you won't have time to worry!

Unknown

Contents

Introduction   **1**

PART 1
Identifying and Controlling Worry

1   Taking a Look at Worry   **7**

2   Analyzing Your Personal Worry Patterns and Styles   **21**

3   Techniques for Dealing with Worry   **35**

4   Focusing Your Attention Away from Worry   **61**

5   Other Considerations in Solving Your Worry Problem   **75**

6   Reducing the Possibility of Worry   **87**

7   Developing Your Personal Plan to Relieve Worry   **101**

PART 2
Addressing Specific Worries

8   Minor Concerns—Past, Present, and Future   **117**

9   Things You Can Control and Things You   **127**
     Can't Control

10   Serious Life Situations and Possible Future   **139**
     Circumstances

11   Global Concerns, Crime, and Safety   **155**

12   Financial Worries   **165**

13   Health Issues   **185**

14   Relationship Issues   **213**

15   Personal Issues   **237**

     Epilogue   **253**

     Resources   **255**

     References   **265**

Introduction

You may never have given much thought to worry. You just did it and never thought much about it. Then one day you realized it was taking its toll on your life—it was taking up too much time and energy. Maybe it was making you sick. So you decided to stop worrying or at least worry less. But you found it wasn't an easy thing not to do. Maybe you've always been aware that you were a worrier and have been looking at ways to stop this intrusion into your life. Or, perhaps worry is not an obsession for you at all—you accept that you'll have anxious reactions to certain stressful situations and that that is part of human nature, but you want to counter some of the unhealthy side effects of worry, such as headaches, snapping at loved ones, or overeating.

I inherited my habit of being a serious worrier from my mother. I've never met anyone who worried as much as my mother did. She worried about things I never even thought about. I wonder if she ever thought about giving up her worry habit. I certainly have thought about giving up mine.

For the last twenty years I have tried to make a conscious effort to stop worrying. I have been somewhat successful. But not as successful as I would like to be. I still catch myself worrying about some highly unlikely, catastrophic event.

I started to try to stop worrying when I realized how much time I spend worrying and how it affects me. Although I never timed it, it was a lot. I was engrossed in worrying at least 25 percent of the time. I estimate that 99.9 percent of the things I've worried about have never happened or have never become serious issues in my life. So I wasted all that time—time

I could have spent looking at the scenery, reading a good book, meditating, making love, or even sleeping (at least half of my worrying takes place at night when I should be sleeping). Worrying also kicks off recurring gastrointestinal problems, increases the likelihood that I will get depressed (or stay depressed), and makes my life and the life of those around me fairly miserable from time to time. Sometimes it has literally made me sick.

I'm one of those highly motivated, growth-oriented people, so I put on my thinking cap to try to figure out how I could get rid of this intrusion in my life. I thought back to a strategy that had helped me deal with another serious issue in my life: For many years I experienced extreme ups and downs of mood that were, with increasing frequency, interfering with the quality of my life. My efforts to find solutions with psychiatric medications were less than fruitful—I had severe side effects with all of them. My determination to improve the quality of my life led me on a search for alternative solutions.

Over several years I conducted an extensive study of how people who experience mood swings and other kinds of psychiatric symptoms reduce these symptoms, get their lives under control, and move on to do the things they want to do. This was where I found my answers. Learning a piece here and a piece there of people's self-help techniques and strategies for dealing with psychiatric symptoms, I began putting them to use in my own life. Gradually the ups and downs of mood became less and less of an issue and, once again, I was enjoying my life. I have written several books on these topics and they have been received positively by people all over the world.

By using these same methods, I thought I might find some answers to my worry problem. I set up another research project, and with a questionnaire (just getting the questionnaire filled out was a big worry for some people), focus groups, and interviews, I have learned how a variety of people deal with worry in their lives. They were studied to find out how much they worry, what they worry about, if and when worry was helpful, how they eliminated worry they didn't want, and how they deal with worry in extremely stressful situations. Many of the participants in this study said the research process itself helped them understand their worry habits, which is the first step towards relief. Their contributions have helped me create a book that will guide you on a journey to help reduce the worry in your life, or change the way you respond to worries so they are easier to manage.

How to Use This Book

This book is different from other books you may have read about worry. While it contains some general facts about worry, its main focus is on relieving your worry. The information on how to do that comes from others who have relieved worry in their own lives. The text will become more individualized as you proceed, helping you to deal with your own worry problem in ways that best suit your style and preferences.

In this book you will be looking at options for dealing with common, everyday worries as well as worries about very serious and even life-threatening issues. Each chapter begins with an italicized quote from a study participant that reinforces a key point. Part 1 includes a general discussion of worry as well as specific techniques for defining, exploring, and controlling your personal worry habits. It follows a model in which understanding your own patterns is a key part of the process. Other steps in the process include practicing relaxation techniques, learning methods for worry control (and finding which ones work best for you), and strengthening your problem-solving skills. Chapter 7 will guide you through the process of developing a personalized plan to relieve worry, based on the methods in this book. Part 2 goes on to explore various general and specific kinds of worry along with a vast array of suggestions, techniques, skills, and strategies that others have used successfully to help relieve worry in their lives. Some may make you exclaim, "What a good idea!" You may respond to others with, "I'd never do that," "That doesn't seem like it would work," or "What a dumb idea." You can give them a try anyway or avoid them altogether. It's up to you. Gravitate toward those you really feel would work well for you.

This is a book about choice. It doesn't tell you what you must do; it gives you a variety of options of what you could do. It may even help you discover other options on your own. You will find that there may be whole sections or chapters you can just skip over because they don't apply to you, they don't interest you, or you don't feel like addressing certain issues right now. Do what feels right to you. You can work through the book from cover to cover or you can use the table of contents as a guide in customizing your personal approach to controlling worry. Work at it while it feels good to you. Then set the book aside and return to it later. Go through it slowly. Give yourself time to assimilate each new thing you learn about yourself.

This is a workbook. While it's hard to forget being scolded about writing in books, write in this book to your heart's content. Writing enriches and reinforces the process. Don't allow yourself to get bogged down in spelling, punctuation, grammar, and sentence structure. You can make up your own rules as you go along, whatever you're comfortable with. It's your book. You can treat it like a diary if you want to. Ask family members and friends to respect your privacy and not read your writings without your permission.

Settle down in a comfortable quiet spot with a favorite writing instrument and get started. Enjoy yourself. Luxuriate in feeling that you are doing something really good for yourself.

PART 1

Identifying and Controlling Worry

1

Taking a Look at Worry

Worry is thinking about something that has
happened, or will happen, in an obsessive way.
Going over something again and again and asking,
"What will I do? What should I have done?"

Worry has been part of the human condition for a long, long time. Did our Cro-Magnon ancestors worry about completing a successful mastodon hunt? Did ancient Egyptians worry about crop failure in a dry year? Probably they did. How far worrying goes back can't be documented, but it's likely that once humans remembered yesterday and anticipated tomorrow, worry became part of life.

In this nation, worry is very much in evidence. A twenty-year study that ended in 1976 suggested that worry was in fact on the rise (Veroff, Douvan, and Kulka 1981). It's a part of our popular culture. "Don't worry, be happy," says Bobby McFerrin in one song. "It takes a worried man to sing a worried song," says another (by the Kingston Trio). We admonish our children or friends to "stop being such a worrywart." American humorist and folk philosopher Mark Twain said, when asked about worry, "I have known a great many troubles, most of which never happened." Advertisements create a market for products that promise to reduce worry, like Celestial Seasonings®—"soothing teas for a nervous world." We are urged to find relief from worry by adding the right food, medication, sport, or hobby to our lives.

Worry is not, however, a uniquely American habit. Many, probably most, cultures acknowledge the presence of worry and develop culturally acceptable ways for dealing with it. In traditional Eastern societies, for example, worry beads are used. Many religious traditions also address worry. In Christian scriptures (Matthew 6:27), for example, Jesus is said to have asked his followers, "Which of you can add one cubit to his stature by worrying?" In Hebrew scriptures (Proverbs 17:22), King Solomon's advice included, "A cheerful heart is good medicine, but a worrisome spirit dries up the bones."

It's important for you to understand that as a worrier, you are not alone. Talking to and interviewing people about their worry has been very validating for me. I have seen that there are many other people out there just like me. And many of them worry about the same things I do, often in the very same way. Just how widespread is worry? It's difficult to give reliable statistics because worry, though a near universal phenomenon, means different things to different people. Results of a survey conducted by Thomas Borkevec of Penn State University indicated that 15 percent of people worry to excess, 30 percent worry very little, and the remaining 55 percent are somewhere in between. Dr. Edward Hallowell of Harvard Medical School puts the worry rates higher than the Penn State study. He states that, in this nation, one in four persons will at some point in life meet the criteria for an anxiety disorder, a treatable condition defined in part by the presence of debilitating worry.

So, although there is no definite way of knowing, I think we can safely assume that more people worry excessively than don't. Perhaps, as I did, you can relate to some of the following worry scenarios that were shared by the people who participated in my worry study:

> Last week I hurt my back and missed two days of work. A week or so prior to that, I was semi-avoiding dealing with a situation at work due to being overwhelmed with other tasks that were simpler to deal with. Well, the avoided situation blew up while I was out sick and maybe could have been handled if I'd done something earlier. I was very worried that I was going to be "called on the carpet" for letting the problem get out of hand. I kept going over in my mind how I was going to handle the confrontation. When I went back to work, it seemed no one thought it was a very big deal. I worried for no apparent reason.

> My husband travels a lot for business purposes. This has always worried me. I tend to go a bit overboard, keeping an eye on the news for word of plane crashes until I hear from him. I have gotten better about this over the years, but I still do it.

I say something I think I shouldn't have said, then I'll replay the moment and worry about it. The next time I see that person I'll say, "You know, I hope I didn't . . ." And they'll usually say, "Sarah, what are you talking about?" Or "No problem!"

Right now I'm working on about ten architectural projects and I don't know how I will ever finish them and keep all the clients happy. This happens every once in a while. I dream of a lottery win so I can give all the money back and stop working. Of course, this never happens—and I always finish all the projects.

My husband, daughter, and I were at my cousin's apartment alone in New York City (we lived in western New York State) at 2 A.M. waiting for our two sons (ages nineteen and twenty-one), who had been expected from Boston, by car, at 10:00. We'd had no call and were in a strange city in which they also did not "know" their way around. I was terrified that they'd been in a car accident and were both killed. *Terrified.* Pacing. Heart-sick. Looking out the window. Trying to calm myself with self-talk. Of course, they arrived safely.

Currently my mother is facing carotid artery surgery. The doctors inform us that she may do well, she may stroke during the operation, or she may not survive. I can't stop expecting the worst. My worrying can neither promote nor prevent any of these options, so . . . why worry?

As you have been reading these worry scenarios, you may have thought of an example from your own life. It might feel good to write it down.

_____

_____

_____

_____

_____

Now that you know that as a worrier, you are not alone, you can move on to examining your worry more closely and making some decisions about what to do about it.

The process of getting a handle on your worrying begins by taking a close look at worry in general. Often, concepts like worry are rather diffuse in your life. It helps to clarify what worry means to you, to define it for yourself. Let's begin the process by answering the questions "What is worry?" "What's wrong with worry?" "What's good about it?" "When does it become a problem?" and "What can you do about it?"

What Is Worry?

Worry seems to mean slightly different things to different people. Hallowell defines worry as a complex type of fear that feeds off both the past and the future, as well as a spiral of doubts and presumptions (1997). For the purposes of his study, Borkevec labeled worry as a sort of uncontrollable mental problem solving that's related to fear (1994). Davey sees worry as part of a problem-solving process that has gone awry (1994). In his view, worry can serve a constructive purpose; but too much worry can do more harm than good. What's clear is that the most important characteristic of worry is *thinking*. In fact, when you're worrying, you're probably thinking too much. In talking with my study participants, I found that they saw worry in many different ways. While there were repeated themes, the variety of definitions was fascinating. It became clear that in order to address a problem with worry, you must not only be familiar with the clinical definition, but you must also know what it means to you.

Here's what a few of the study participants said:

Worry is somewhere between *concern*, which is a milder (perhaps earlier) form of worry, and *anxiety*, which might be a more intense version of worry. Anxiety you feel in the stomach or in your breathing, while worry is more mental.

Worry is tension or repetitive thinking about things in unproductive ways.

Worry is either a chronic or acute concern, about which you may or may not be able to do anything, which may or may not be realistic, and which may or may not be troublesome and or self-destructive.

The U.S. English Thesaurus says worry is "to torment oneself with disturbing thoughts." A study participant said, "To my mind, 'torment' may be a bit strong, but it separates worry from concern." The thesaurus defines worry as synonymous with anxiety, apprehension, concern, fear, care, disquiet, uneasiness, misgiving, and solicitude. Do you agree with any of those synonyms? If so, which ones?

Key descriptions of worry that were most consistently mentioned by study participants include the following:

- Undesirable

- Troublesome

- Disturbing

- Unproductive

- Obsessive

- Repetitive

- Anxiety producing

- Habitual

- Dominating

- Preoccupying

- Negative

- Tension inducing

- Frustrating

Based on what you've read so far and what you know from your experiences, write your own definition of worry. It can be simple and concise or much more complex—whatever clearly describes worry for you.

Is Worry the Same as Anxiety?

While worry is a component of most anxiety disorders, it is not necessarily the same thing as anxiety. In the cognitive behavioral model, worry involves thoughts, and anxiety involves emotions. You can think of it as a sort of cognitive behavioral continuum where worry is at one end and anxiety is at the other. The intensity, frequency, and urgency of a worry can push you along the continuum towards anxiety. Depending on what you're worrying about, worry can also lead to depression, shame, shyness, or panic. It is most often associated with generalized anxiety disorder, which is characterized by having excessive worry and anxiety for more days than not over an extended period of time (APA 1994). One key characteristic that sets worry apart from anxiety is that worry is generally a much more thought out process. The worrier often creates a whole story or scenario based on the threat of a possible future event. Tallis, Davey, and Capuzzo have described this as the "narrative quality" of worry (1994, 63). Many researchers believe that worry might actually be a misguided way for you to avoid anxiety, because when you worry, you are attempting to prepare yourself for a potentially anxiety-provoking situation.

What's Wrong with Worry?

Now that you've defined what worry means to you, what's wrong with it? Why would you want to stop worrying or reduce your level of worry? Again, the answers to this question from study participants were as varied as the people who took part in the study. But first let's look at a quote from *Conversations with God: An Uncommon Dialogue.*

> . . . most people worry themselves to death.
>
> Worry is just about the worst form of mental activity there is—next to hate, which is deeply self-destructive. Worry is pointless. It is wasted mental energy. It also creates bio-chemical reactions which harm the body, producing everything from indigestion to coronary arrest, and a multitude of things in between.
>
> Health will improve almost at once when worrying ends. (Walsch 1996, 187–190)

One woman in the study said,

> Worry/fear prevents me from making good decisions. I also believe that a prolonged state of fear/worry has negative effects on health. When I was worried about problems with my husband's first wife, I actually developed heart symptoms!

Another study participant said,

> Personally, I get scared, depressed, or sick and can't stay in a high worry state without it progressing.

The Negative Effects of Worry on Your Body and Mind

Worry can be the cause of much physical discomfort. It has been known to be responsible for headaches, stomachaches, sleeplessness, and fatigue. The most noted physical response is that of increased muscle tension. Studies have also shown that worry can negatively affect memory, attention, and information processing (Mathews 1990). The idea is that because you're busy thinking about your worries, your capacity to focus on these other cognitive functions is decreased. In my case, constant worrying has a big impact on my sleeping pattern and digestive system.

What physical and mental changes do you experience as a result of your worrying?

_____

_____

The following ideas from study participants may help you understand how worry makes other people feel and why reducing or eliminating worry from your life is an important action to take. Read through the list and check off the statements you agree with.

Worry

_____ is a terrible drain.

_____ gets in the way of trust.

_____ makes me feel powerless.

_____ wastes a lot of time and energy.

_____ "turns off" others.

_____ sometimes prevents action.

_____ is counterproductive.

_____ is debilitating.

_____ causes physical symptoms like dizziness, nausea, headaches, and insomnia.

_____ opposes feelings of trust, serenity, confidence, courage, being in the moment, acceptance, and peace.

In your view, what's wrong with worrying?

_____

_____

_____

_____

_____

_____

What's Good about Worry?

After reading the first sections of this chapter, you might be thinking, *"Are their any positive aspects of worry?"* Well, believe it or not, there are. But sometimes it's not easy to know which aspects of worry are the ones you might want to preserve.

One study participant said,

> Since I view "worries" as signposts, I respect the nature of their gift. I'm not going out to sign up for any extra ones, but my "worries"/concerns are a vital part of my life. To the extent they serve a purpose, I'll use them for good . . . and let them go.

Several others said rather emphatically that worry has NO value. One said, "It's hard to see the benefits of something I tend to view as a waste of time and energy." However, while most of us wish we didn't worry, many of the people who participated in the study did agree that there are, in fact, positive aspects to this "worrisome" condition.

Worry is an adaptive process; that is, if you can control it, you can get it to work *for* you instead of *against* you. Just as stress can have a positive or negative impact on your life, so can worry. Stress researcher Hans Selye refers to this positive stress as "eustress." While no term has yet to be agreed upon for the good kind of worry, we can think of it as "wise worry." When you're using worry to your benefit, it can prepare and motivate you.

A friend of mine feels that

> Being unpleasantly concerned about something is often beneficial if it stimulates us to do something about whatever it is that is worrying us, or even if it just puts into focus for us what we really care about. When I worry about someone else I'm expressing some lack of confidence in them as well as the fact that I care about them. Worry is like going to the dentist—it's an unpleasant experience that sometimes is a necessary part of things getting better.

Here's what some of my study participants said:

> I worry as little as anyone I know, but I think that to never worry is to be not fully human. After all, there are problems in life that don't get resolved easily, that can't be denied.

> Whatever I may think (negatively) about worry as a part of my life, I realize most of the time there's a kernel of truth or a lesson to be learned or a wake-up call in there somewhere.

> If I didn't worry at all, there are things I would never follow through on—like doctor's appointments, etc. It can be a positive force in creating enough discomfort to make necessary changes.

Worry that is the result of an awareness, naming, and owning of a concern or problem can result in healthy responses. Worry can galvanize me into creative and corrective action in the face of a problem. I believe that a degree of worry is essential for a whole and healthy life.

The following list is made up of the positive aspects of worry identified by my study participants. Looking at their ideas may help you decide what, for you, are the positive aspects of worry. Check off the phrases that you agree with.

Worry is useful when it

_____ provides motivation to take a necessary action or to make a necessary change.

_____ helps you realize there are problems and directs you toward solving them.

_____ is an avenue for exploration of possibilities.

_____ inspires creative thought relative to the problem.

_____ helps solve problems.

_____ helps us see something we need to do or take care of.

_____ creates positive change.

_____ causes reassessment of a situation.

_____ is used "to digest an issue," to analyze it in detail.

_____ reminds you that you have a choice.

_____ encourages the search for new information.

_____ reminds us to use caution.

_____ warns of danger.

_____ encourages preparation for a possible outcome.

_____ warns of a necessary change in attitude.

_____ inspires preparation for upcoming events or tasks.

_____ causes serious scrutiny of an important issue.

_____ serves as an early warning sign of depression or some other physical or emotional problem, facilitating early intervention.

When is worry useful for you?

_____

_____

_____

_____

_____

_____

When Does Worry Become a Problem?

In *Thoughts & Feelings,* McKay, Davis, and Fanning state that you have a serious problem with worry if you

- are chronically anxious about future dangers or threats.

- consistently make negative predictions about the future.

- often overestimate the probability or seriousness of bad things happening.

- can't stop repeating the same worries over and over.

- escape worry by distracting yourself or avoiding certain situations.

- find it difficult to use worry constructively to produce solutions to problems.

Seriously worried people find it difficult to control their worry and typically experience these symptoms:

- Restlessness

- Fatigue

- Difficulty concentrating

- Irritability

- Muscle tension

- Sleep disturbance

The point at which worry becomes a problem differs for everyone. I realized worry was a problem for me when I noticed how much time I wasted worrying about things that never happened, how terrible I felt when

I was worrying, and that worry might be a cause, rather than a result of, depression.

A young woman in the study said her awareness of the role of worry in her mother's life helped her identify the point at which worry became a problem for her. She describes her mother as an obsessive worrier. She said,

> People began ignoring my mother. Rather than do something about her worry problem, my mother chose to intensify the fretfulness and change her definition of successful attention. Now if you lose your temper and yell at her because she is saying the same thing over and over, she is still getting your attention even if it's not in a positive way for anybody.
>
> I found it so annoying and unattractive and unhappy and I guess I looked at it from the point of view of how unhappy she was making all the people around her. I didn't want to be the kind of person who made all the people around me unhappy and angry with me. That's when I decided to take some direct action to eliminate my own problem with worry.

Now consider the responses to the question "When does worry become a problem for you?" from participants in the worry study:

> Worry is a problem when it does more harm than good. Worry generally indicates a problem; it's part of my way of responding to problems. The worry itself becomes a problem when it becomes the object of worry itself. For example, I sometimes find myself worried about something that seems to me inconsequential or that I am not in a position to do anything about. I may be obsessed at work with the thought, "Did I leave the coffee-maker on at home?" even though I doubt that a fire would result even if I did leave it on, and even though there's nothing I can do about it until I go back home. When the worrisome thoughts continue anyway, then they themselves become something to worry about. "Why can't I stop thinking about this stuff?"

> Worry is a problem when it interferes with living a full, rich life and when my self-expression is compromised.

> When the thought is the last at night and the first of the morning.

> When I feel helpless to do anything, then I feel the grinding in my stomach, I waken thinking of my troubles, and I have a hard time relaxing.

> When it haunts me every day, when I hang onto my worry instead of doing something about it.

When I feel overwhelmed or when I'm fretting over some decision and going back and forth on it.

When it offers nothing to the solution of a problem and begins to complicate the real issues.

When it interferes with constructively solving life's problems.

When I can't stop the repetitive thought processes and resolve the situation and when I become so obsessed with the issue that I can't focus on anything else properly.

Worry becomes a problem for me when I notice that no matter what I'm doing during the day, for example laundry, cooking, driving, reading, working, or talking with other people, my mind continually comes back to the object of my worry. It almost seems like the thoughts of worry are beyond my control. I get frustrated and angry with myself.

Worry becomes a problem when it prevents me from making good decisions.

When my daily functioning is disturbed; i.e., eating, recreation, sleep, work, etc., and when this occurs for an extended period of time—a week or more in my book.

Worry becomes a problem

- when my stomach is tight and I cannot eat—if I get upset or acid stomach, then I am in extreme worry.

- if I become tense and very abrasive or argumentative.

- if I become depressed.

Many people reported sleep as being an indicator, or one of several indicators, that worry has become a problem.

There are two indicators that worry is becoming a problem for me. One is when I wake up in the middle of the night and can't get back to sleep. This, of course, compounds the problem, as I'm now also worrying about not getting enough sleep for what I have to deal with the next day. The other is when I can't focus my attention on other things and keep coming back in my thoughts to the worry.

When I can't get to sleep at night, I know I have a problem. When I discuss a problem incessantly with friends, it can become "too much."

When it gets in the way of living one's life, either in or out of bed. One can lose wakefulness, as well as sleep, as a result of worry.

Worry can prompt fear, and that fear might prevent action. Worry can close a person down.

When worry is causing sleeplessness, physical symptoms such as shortness of breath and stomach cramps, absentmindedness and an inability to follow through with work, then I know I have to do something about it.

Worry becomes a problem when it ceases to be attached to a specific, alterable issue. When I am greatly stressed, my worry becomes comprehensive; and I know I am in the danger zone when I go into "attack mode" to conquer my worries, losing both sleep and weight in the exhaustive process.

I know my worry has gotten to be "too much" when people say, "Lighten up." When I can't sleep I *know* it's become serious, because nothing ever disturbs my sleep.

I'm on worry overload when I

- dwell on the specific concern and do not think about other issues I should be dealing with.

- am unable to sleep.

- try to read a book or article and keep thinking about the concern.

Worry definitely becomes a problem when I can't get to sleep or find myself waking up in the middle of the night. It's also a problem when I can't be consoled by friends over what I'm worried about.

When I can't sleep or I begin to overeat to calm down, I know worry is the culprit.

Worry is a problem when it affects life's pleasures and when I awaken very early and can't get back to sleep.

I know worry is getting to me when

- my focus is on a specific concern to the extent that I have difficulty in moving ahead in my work.

- I remain awake, unable to fall asleep for two or more consecutive nights. I then worry about becoming exhausted from not being able to sleep.

- I reach the point of being immobilized.

Worry becomes a problem for me when it interferes with my daily life. My concentration is poor. It's hard to sleep. I may not want to eat or I may want to eat the wrong things.

Several people said, "Worrying is always a problem." Their reasons may be useful to you as you define the point at which worry becomes a problem for you:

Being concerned is often realistic, but too much worry is a disturbance of the mind. It's a negative thing and anything negative is basically unhealthy.

Any significant degree of worry is a problem. Worry is negative thinking and negative thinking is not good.

When does worry become a problem for you?

_____

_____

_____

_____

_____

_____

What Can You Do?

When dealing with worry, there are two basic options: You can attempt to control your environment or you can attempt to control how you react to your environment. In most cases, the latter will probably be easier. To say that it is easier to control your reactions than it is to control your environment, however, is not to say that controlling yourself will be easy. It is hard work, and you need to give yourself permission to make mistakes before you get the hang of it.

The problem of too much worry can be approached from many different directions. One way might work best for you, while a different combination of solutions might work best for someone else. Some find that therapy helps. Others find that medications such as Prozac and Zoloft, along with therapy, provide the boost they need to get past their worries. If you are interested in learning about these medications and whether or not they're right for you, consult your physician for advice. Still others find that simple life changes are enough to provide the relief they need.

Since, according to Barlow and Kraske, worry is composed of three major components—thoughts, behavior, and physiology—those are the areas you'll need to focus on to do something about your problem with worry (1994). The chapters that follow will address these different components of worry and provide exercises to help you understand, address, and alleviate your worry. So, read on to find your own solutions.

2

Analyzing Your Personal Worry Patterns and Styles

In my family we didn't check out whether our worries were real, we quietly behaved as though they were. I have learned better skills now, but under stress I can still feel the pull of old habits.

Before you can begin to solve your problem with worry, you must first understand your worry habit. This means looking into the where, what, when, and why. Answering these questions may not be easy for you, but once you've done this you'll be able to identify your weak spots and learn how to strengthen them.

Where Does Your Worrying Come From?

An important part of analyzing your worry pattern involves looking into the origin of your habit. For some, worrying has been a lifelong pattern. For others, it may have begun as the result of a traumatic or disappointing event or as part of a treatable condition. Figuring out the source won't change the fact that you worry, but it might help you decide which is the best way to approach the problem.

Do you see yourself as someone who has always been a worrier?

_____ Yes

_____ No

If you answered yes, explain why you think this. Describe things you do and ways you act that support this.

_____

_____

_____

_____

If you answered no, can you pinpoint when your worrying began? Did it coincide with any specific event or sequence of events in your life?

_____

_____

Do you see your worry habit as part of your personality ("I'm just a nervous person")?

_____

Do you think you "learned" how to worry from others? If so, whom?

_____

_____

Family Worry Patterns

Regardless of whether their worrying began as the result of a specific event or has been a lifelong trait, many people feel that worry patterns in their family of origin strongly affect their worry habit and, in many cases, make that habit a difficult one to break.

My mother had a severe problem with worry that she was never able to break. Much of her worry was focused on things, issues, or people over which she had no control—most often her adult children and grandchildren. She responded to her worry by devising grand schemes that she was sure, if implemented, would help them to overcome what she saw as huge problems in their lives. Often, they did not agree that the "issues" were really problems, and I can't remember when anyone ever actually implemented one of her grand schemes. I remember when she called me and told me that the solution to the problems she perceived my brother and my nephew as having would be corrected if they planted a huge garden and gave all the produce to homeless shelters. Since neither of them had any interest in agriculture, I thought her idea had little merit. I shared that feeling with her but to no avail. She persisted in fruitlessly trying to get them to pursue this route.

I feel strongly that my mother unwittingly passed her worry habit on to me. While I have given up on developing grand schemes for my children or grandchildren, my worry habit persists and demands constant attention to hold it at bay. Along with my brothers and sisters, I have noticed that my father, who had never been a worrier, took over my mother's role as family worrier after her death.

Study participants had a great deal to say about the influence of family worry patterns.

> Oh yes. My mother was a great worrier. I think as an only child, I was able to see how futile and unhelpful the worry she focused on me was. I did, however, latch onto and carry into my own life her worry about entertaining.

> As anxious as I am, I'm a calm spring day compared to my family of origin. Everything was shame—shame and depravity, from morals to material goods. There isn't enough goodness or bounty, so you must be watchful and frugal. My parents cut paper napkins in half; now they cut them in quarters. According to them, you can't afford to make any mistakes

> I do have choices about whether I worry or not, but it is an ingrained habit.

> I couldn't not worry. It's related to my value system. In my family there was a direct relationship between worry and values and beliefs.

> I used to think worry was part of being responsible.

> There are optimists and pessimists. I developed optimism. I did not consciously develop it. It was just there. My son picked it up from me.

> In my village it was normal to worry but not to be happy.

> I learned that I was more sensitive if I worried.

> In my family, the styles of worry varied as much as the topics.

> My parents used worry to control my behavior. They'd make me feel bad by saying things like, "We were up half the night worrying about you."

> Once when I told my father not to worry, as I was going off on a cross-country hitchhiking trip, he told me, "It's a father's job to worry."

Do you feel your worry is influenced by family worry patterns? If so, describe the patterns and how you think they were passed down to you.

_____

_____

_____

_____

_____

_____

Is Worry a State of Being for You?

When you're learning to cope better with worry, it helps to take a look at its role in your life. Is it a significant feature or is it just a pesky annoyance from time to time? Through the study we discovered that there are two kinds of worriers: those for whom worry is a state of being, and those who only worry about specific concerns. For the first group, worry is more or less a constant or habitual state. One study participant described her mother as a person who is constantly in a state of worry—she is always worried, but it may not be about anything significant or anything at all. Another described himself as a "specific concerns" worrier only:

> For me, worry is related to specific events or concerns—so there will come an end to that worry.

> When I was younger, I would have considered myself a "worried person." I lived in a chronic state of tension, fearful of what might happen next. For me it was a state of being. Through the years I have worked hard at changing that way of being. Now, although I still worry much more than I think is healthy, my worry is almost always related to specific concerns, the kind of worry that is over when the concern is addressed. I got past having worry be a state of being for me by using the kinds of strategies described in this book.

A number of people said that worry is sometimes a state of being and at other times it is related to specific concerns. Many of those people said that worry was a significant feature of their work life but not of their personal life. For instance,

I worry more in my professional life because I get paid to anticipate problems.

Others felt the opposite was true, that, as I do, they worry more about their personal life than about their work life.

I know I do my job well, so I'm not worried about that. It's my social skills I'm not so sure about.

Do you feel that worry is a significant feature of your life?

_____ Yes

_____ No

Explain your answer.

_____

_____

_____

_____

Do you feel you are always in a chronic state of worry?

_____ Yes

_____ No

If you answered yes, describe how that affects you and your quality of life.

_____

_____

_____

_____

Do you restrict your worries to specific concerns?

_____ Yes

_____ No

If you answered yes, describe how that affects you and your quality of life:

_____

_____

_____

_____

Do your answers to the preceding questions suggest some change you would like to make in your life?

_____ Yes

_____ No

If you answered yes, please describe this change.

_____

_____

_____

_____

Do you think you could implement this change now?

_____ Yes

_____ No

If you answered yes, how could you do it? Are there steps you'd need to take?

_____

_____

_____

_____

If you don't think you could do it now, why not?

_____

_____

Perhaps in working through the rest of this book, you can discover how you could make this change.

Do You Have Control over How Much You Worry?

Most people in the study felt that they have significant control over how much they worry when they work at it. Sometimes one's age or life situation make it easier to control worry.

> Absolutely! It does, however, take vigor to be aware of where one's thoughts are going. It's like pulling weeds out ASAP.

> I've lived long enough and had enough problems to know that things eventually work out.

> Because my life is so much fun, it's relatively easy for me to let go of what are mostly concerns based on pure speculation!

Others felt they have some, but not complete, control over how much they worry.

> I can sometimes control my worry. I think it's natural for humans to be concerned about their situation, about others, etc. How strongly worry affects one's life is where we have some control. If it disrupts my daily functioning, then I feel I need to make changes—and I do. I do not avoid going through pain to try to fool myself into thinking that avoidance will be easier.

> If I'm in my danger zone of stress, I almost don't have any control over my worry. If I'm relaxed to moderate, I control it very well.

> I'm getting better at controlling my response to worry, but I haven't got a great deal of control over my worry capacity. I don't know if I would want to change my sensitivity to worry, because that seems to be related to compassion and concern. But I would like to know how to address and relieve worry when it comes up.

> Sometimes I can let it go just by realizing it's a useless thing to think about. Sometimes it's a recurring theme, and I can't stop thinking about it.

How much control do you have over how much you worry?

_____ I can almost always control my worry.

_____ Sometimes I can control my worry.

_____ It's very difficult for me ever to control how much I worry.

If you don't have as much control over your worry as you would like, what do you think you could do about it?

_____

_____

_____

_____

When Do You Worry?

Many of the study participants reported that they worried more in times of general stress. When asked at what specific time of day they worry most, several said they often lie awake at night worrying about some future event. Figuring out when you worry in general and at what time of day you're more susceptible to worry can help you decide when is the best time to take action towards worry control.

Are there times in your life when you worry more than usual? For example, during times of general stress, overwork, or mild depression.

_____

_____

Do you find that worry tends to precede or follow particular types of interactions or situations? If so, which ones?

_____

_____

When do you worry most often during the day?

_____

What Do You Worry About?

What you worry about is as much a part of your worry pattern as how often you do it. As you saw in the previous section, some people only worry about their personal lives, while others worry more about their work lives. We found that many people in the study could easily name what they worried about most.

> I worry a lot about what other people think of me. Most of my worries are in some way connected to that.

I work for myself. Even though my business has been consistently very successful, I worry about having enough work, which means money, to make ends meet. Along with that worry, I worry about being capable of doing the work necessary to make the money to make ends meet. Add to that the worry that someday, someone will notice that I'm not really good at what I do.

Most of my worries are focused on the people I love the most—my family and very close friends. My kids—all well into adulthood—are capable and competent, yet I worry about everything from their health and safety to their love affairs and happiness. I worry a lot more about others than about myself.

When it comes to the day-to-day annoyances, I don't worry much. It's the big stuff that really gets me. Like the prospect of one of those missiles aimed in our direction inadvertently getting set off. Or about an accident at the nuclear power plant in a neighboring town. And what about that smog that has hung over the downtown area for the last few weekends? And is this unseasonably warm weather here to stay? Is the East Coast really going to be flooded in the next few years? I could go on and on.

Do you tend to worry more about situations involving yourself, or yourself in relation to others? Or do you worry more about what's going on with other people?

_____

_____

Using the following list, choose which issues you worry about most. Your answers will help you decide which chapters in part 2 will be most helpful for you.

_____ Minor concerns, such as what to have for lunch, being on time, or having a bad hair day

_____ Things you can control

_____ Things you can't control

_____ Serious situations

_____ The future

_____ Global concerns

_____ Financial concerns

_____ Health and safety issues

_____ Relationship issues

_____ Personal issues

When you're ready to move on to part 2, look over the table of contents to see which chapters correspond to your most serious worry problems.

Why Do You Worry?

I saved the hardest question for last. The answer to this question is not as simple as "Because something might go wrong." The answer you're looking for here is the reason (or reasons) behind your worry—that is, what worrying does for you. People worry about a variety of issues for a variety of reasons. But, in general, the reasons people worry can be broken down into the following five categories (Borkevec 1994). Each reason is followed by quotes from study participants who identified with that reason.

1. Superstitious avoidance of an event.

This is like telling yourself, "If I worry about it happening, it's less likely to happen."

> If I worry enough to name it and affirm its presence, it loses its power over me.

> I feel like if I think about it a lot, there's no way it can happen. Maybe there's some greater power that decides that because I've put so much energy into thinking about something, it'll go easy on me.

2. Practical avoidance of an event.

This is like telling yourself, "If I worry about it happening, I'll figure out a way to prevent it."

> When I worry about things going wrong at work, for example, I usually try to fix the problem before my worries can come true. I suppose worry can be helpful in that way.

> If I let myself worry about something enough, I'll get so worried that I give myself no choice but to do something about it. Often I'll spend a lot of time playing out different scenarios in my head. If I do this for long enough I can usually come up with a way to avoid the problem altogether.

3. Avoidance of an emotion.

This is like telling yourself, "If I worry about this event happening, I won't have to think about what I'm really feeling."

I remember when my father was really sick—in the hospital actually—I was obsessed with how my son was doing in school. He'd gotten a C in one class, and it was all I could think about. Looking back on the whole experience, I think it was just easier for me to focus on my son than it was to think about the possibility of my father dying.

Whenever I get upset about something at work, I decide it's time to redecorate my home or start doing community service. I worry about anything that'll take my mind off of what I should be worrying about.

4. Preparation for an event.

This is like telling yourself, "If I worry about this event happening, I will be prepared to deal with it when it does happen."

Especially with anticipatory anxiety about public performances, the more I worry the better I seem to play.

I have a friend who will create the worst possible scenario. When the actual event happens, it's almost refreshing because it's nothing compared to what she had conjured up.

5. Motivation for action.

This is like telling yourself, "If I worry about this event happening, I will be more inclined to do something to prevent or change the predicted outcome."

I don't believe that worry has any major preventative features *except* in the area of practical health and safety measures. Worry about health can lead to diet modifications, more exercise, etc.

The worry doesn't necessarily prevent the happening, but thinking about it may actually get me to do something.

Some of these reasons are self-reinforcing. For example, if worrying about an upcoming deadline does get you to do your work, you are telling yourself that worry is indeed effective as a motivational tool.

Which of these reasons do you identify with? If you don't feel that any of them have to do with your worrying, can you think of your own reason?

Do you see your worry mostly as preventive in nature or avoidant?

_____

If you chose "preventive," do you think it's possible to save the preventive aspects of your worry while alleviating its harmful effects? How? If you chose "avoidant," do you think it's possible for you to face issues in order to alleviate the harmful effects of worry? How?

_____

_____

_____

_____

Are You Willing to Work on Your Worry?

Getting down to the bottom line, how much time, energy, and expense are you willing to invest in controlling your worry habit? Most people feel like this person, who said,

> If you've got the purgative, I'll gladly pay up for a crate. Worry is the most non-productive, energy-wasting, joy-robbing thing I do.

Here are some echoes of this sentiment:

> I'd spend a lot of time, energy, and money to get rid of worry. It's important to all aspects of your health.

> I have spent a lot of time, etc., in dealing with worry—and feel that I am being very successful with it. I understand where it comes from and how to get rid of it.

> I'm willing to spend considerable spiritual energy to give up the illusion that my fretting is helpful.

> I'd be willing to spend as much time letting go of worry as I do now worrying—which is quite a bit—and more than that.

> I have been willing to take advantage of any tool, exercise, or place that feels right to me as a means of helping me address worry in my life.

> As much time/energy/expense as I can to get rid of worry. My major worry is that whatever I am concerned about will cause a severe depression.

Some people distinguished among kinds of worry, or what else is going on in life, when it came to how much time, energy, and expense they'd be willing to devote.

> I'd spend quite a bit of time, energy, and expense if the worry were severe enough to verge on depression, but not if they're minor worries I can deal with through awareness.

> Letting go of worry is an ongoing life process. The amount of time, energy, or expense changes over time depending on where I am in the process and what situations are presented.

> It depends on the worry. There are the ones where I've done what I can, but still feel tormented—those worries I'd love to give up. I'd spend as much time and energy as the worry depletes me of.

Some say they would, as in the past, continue to invest a lot of time, energy, and money into letting go of worry:

> I have already invested a couple of hours a week for ten years in cognitive therapy. The rewards of the changes I have made so far have been well worth the investment of time and energy, and I believe I still have much work to do.

> I already invest a lot and expect to continue.

Many people said they were willing to put some energy into getting rid of worry, but they didn't have much time or money to put into it.

Now that you've had a chance to consider the kind of investment others are willing to make in relieving worry, how do you feel?

To relieve my worrying I would be willing to invest

Time: ____ A lot ____ Some ____ Little

Energy: ____ A lot ____ Some ____ Little

Money: ____ A lot ____ Some ____ Little

Consider carefully what your answers to these questions mean to you. For instance, if you would be willing to spend a lot of time and energy, and perhaps, but not necessarily, at least some money in relieving your worry problem, then the rest of this book is for you. If you would be willing to invest even some time, energy, and money, again, proceed with the rest of this book, but you may want to be selective about how you proceed. Read the chapter and section headings and proceed with those sections that you feel would be most helpful. If you are not willing to invest anything in relieving your worry, perhaps you should put this book away for the time being, or even give it to a friend; we have found that it does take some time and energy to get rid of worry. If you have money available, that's helpful, but not at all necessary.

3

Techniques for Dealing with Worry

Worry is unavoidable.
It's how you deal with it that you can control.

In this chapter, you'll find a variety of techniques that people in the study have used successfully to control worry. Rather than divert your attention from the worry, they help you relieve the worry by addressing it. (In chapter 4, "Focusing Your Attention Away from Worry," techniques for diverting, distracting, and refocusing yourself will be discussed.) The techniques are separated into two categories: thinking techniques and action techniques. Peruse the headings and see which techniques interest you. Then try them out and see which ones work for you. Some may work well and others may not. You can use those that work well on an ongoing basis to control the worry in your life.

Thinking Techniques

Focusing

Focusing helps me
get to what's underneath it all.

Focusing is a simple, safe, free, non-invasive, yet powerful, self-help technique that several people in the study reported helps target and reduce worry. I have used this technique for several years and agree that it is an effective tool in relieving worry as well as in achieving overall wellness. The focusing sequence uses a series of well-defined questions or steps to help focus on the "real" worry, the one of most importance at a given time. It may be different from what you think the real worry is. For instance, you may feel worried about an upcoming job interview, when in fact the real worry has to do with lack of self-confidence. Once the key issue is identified, focusing helps you connect with the feelings generated by that issue. When you explore your feelings, the result is an understanding at a new level, which translates into a positive change in feeling, and often, reduction of worry.

Focusing is not the same as meditation. The use of one does not preclude use of the other. In meditation, achieving stillness or an emptying of the mind is the goal. In focusing, you feel, respond, and gain insight.

As with any new wellness or growth-oriented technique, the more you practice it, the easier and more effective it becomes. I try to focus at least once a day, addressing issues that are troubling in order to keep them from becoming overwhelming. I do focusing exercises more often when worries seem to be obsessive and keeping me from feeling well. Sometimes I even focus on something really good that has happened so I can linger for a time with those good feelings.

Focusing can provide

- Clarity around an issue

- Direction

- Increased feelings of calmness and relaxation

- Help in preventing distraction by less important issues

- Feelings of overall relief

- A shift in feelings around an issue

- A new level of understanding

One woman reported that she used focusing when she found herself irrationally worried about an upcoming trip. She had traveled extensively in the past and enjoyed it, so she couldn't figure out why she was so worried about this trip. In the focusing exercise she learned that it wasn't really the trip that was making her so apprehensive, but a visit with a difficult relative that she had included as part of the trip. When she explored her feelings around the visit to the relative, she got an image of sinister-looking sharp points coming in her direction. She discovered that her worries were really related to this relative's tendency to wound her with critical comments. As she worked with this new level of understanding, she noticed some relief in the worry. She was able to address the worry more directly and actually decided not to visit the unpleasant relative.

The following are some focusing instructions. They can be refined any way you choose to meet your individual needs. Have a person you trust, and with whom you feel safe, slowly read the instructions to you, giving you time between each step to follow the instructions in your mind and body. You do not have to say anything to the reader. Your responses are your own. If no one is available, record the instructions, again allowing time for your thoughts, and play the tape to yourself when you want to do a focusing exercise. You may choose to write your responses to each step as you go along. I use focusing so much that I have memorized the instructions.

1. Get ready for your focusing exercise by settling down in a comfortable space and asking yourself, "How do I feel inside my body right now?" Search around inside your body to notice any feelings of uneasiness or discomfort and focus your attention on these feelings for a few moments.

2. Ask yourself, "What's between me and feeling fine?" Don't answer; let the feeling or thought that comes in your body do the answering. As each concern comes up, put it aside, like making a mental list. Ask yourself, "Except for these things, am I fine?"

3. Review the list you've made in your mind. See which problem stands out. Which one seems to be begging for your attention? It may be different from the one you thought was most important. Ask yourself if it's okay to focus on the problem. If the answer is yes, notice what you sense in your body when you recall the whole of that problem. (If the answer is no, choose another problem that stands out and let the other alone for the time being.) Sense the whole feeling of the problem. Really feel it in your body for several minutes—focus on every part of it.

4. Let a word, phrase, or image that matches the feeling of this problem come into your mind. For example, a freight train hurtling down a track might signify how you feel about your family coming

to visit. A vase that has many cracks might signify your reaction to a deadline at work.

5. Go back and forth between the word, phrase, or image and the feeling in your body. Do they really match? If they don't, find another word, phrase, or image that does feel like a match. When they match, go back and forth several times between the word, phrase, or image and the feeling in your body. If the feeling in your body changes, follow it with your attention—notice how it changes. Be with the whole of that feeling for several moments.

6. If you want, ask yourself the following questions; this may help you change the way you feel:

   • How does the worst of this feel in my body?

   • What needs to happen inside me for this whole thing to change?

   • What would feel like a small step forward with all this?

   • What would feel like a breath of fresh air in this whole thing?

   • How would it feel inside if this were all okay?

   • What needs to change inside me for this to feel better?

7. Be with the feelings that came up for a few moments. Then ask yourself, "Am I ready to stop or should I do another round of focusing?" If you are going to stop, relax for a few minutes and notice how your feelings have changed before resuming your regular activities.

If you tried focusing, describe how it helped, or did not help, relieve your worry.

_____

_____

_____

_____

There are several books about focusing listed in the resources section at the end of the book.

Guided Imagery

> *Guided imagery worked for me. I'm no longer afraid I'm going to be an incessant worrier like my mother.*

In guided imagery, you use your imagination to direct your focus in a way that is relaxing and healing. The following example is Sheila's guided imagery success story.

> Until I learned guided imagery exercises, I spent a lot of time worrying. I'm sure I learned this from my mother who frets and frets and frets about things she has no control over. Her worry is not resolving the situation and it only makes her and the people around her exasperated and unhappy. It affects the people around her because she is very vocal and repetitive and it gets so frustrating. She seems to be seeking advice or comfort, but when it's given she ignores it and just keeps repeating the worry. When I'm with her I end up feeling angry and frustrated. Sometimes it's frightening because it feels like I might get sucked into it somehow, a sort of contagious anxiety. I found it so annoying and unattractive and unhappy and I guess I looked at it from the point of view of how unhappy she was making all the people around her and I didn't want to be the kind of person who made all the people around me unhappy and angry with me.

Having been so closely involved with her mother's worry as she was growing up, it's clear why, when Sheila began to notice that her own worry patterns looked frighteningly like her mother's, she was so willing and anxious to invest time and money in controlling her worry. She sought out a counselor who had been trained to teach guided imagery. Working with the counselor on a week-to-week basis for a year, and reinforcing the teaching in her daily activities, Sheila now feels that she is in charge, that she has her worry habit under control and will not follow in her mother's footsteps.

The following is Sheila's description of a typical guided imagery exercise that deals with her lack of trust in her own abilities. These worries were wrapped up with fear of the unknown and her perceived lack of ability to smoothly deal with whatever comes up. She says the following exercise helped her deal with worries as minor as putting zippers in pillows or as major as applying for a job change:

> I close my eyes and take several deep cleansing breaths. I then tell myself that the worry is a useless activity because it is not getting me any closer to solving whatever it is I'm worried about. I think of what I was worried about as a deep canyon or a chasm that I have to get across, because I won't make any progress until I get across. I envision a very rickety bridge going across the chasm, but tell myself that, even though it's scary, I have to get across. Pacing back and forth along the side of the canyon isn't doing any good, and the quicker I cross, the quicker I will be moving forward. Then I

slowly and carefully picture myself striding confidently across the bridge, effectively meeting the challenge I was so worried about.

When you're doing your guided imagery, try to come up with a physical image that represents the change you are going to make. It may be walking down a path that's scary, as in the Wizard of Oz. You may be going through the woods but the path of worry just takes you around and around in circles, and you don't get anywhere until you picture yourself getting off that path and following another path—a path that will get you through the woods and out to the other side. The new path might look straight and bright rather than winding and dark. You might use the light at the end of the tunnel image or sunlight. You can visualize mile markers on this path so you get a sense of making progress. The most important point is that this path must be taking you to something or through something instead of around and around something.

For some people, worry may be immobilizing. Guided visualizations create movement, or at least a sense of movement, that helps even if the things that are worrying you are things that cannot be dealt with quickly or are out of your control—for example, whether your daughter got into college, whether you are getting the promotion or the mortgage, learning the results of the biopsy, waiting for the results of your AIDS test, wondering whether someone is going to make it through surgery or whether the chemotherapy will work, and whether your child will continue to "act out" and get worse.

> The guided imagery is active. It gives you something to do, if only in your mind, because you see yourself getting somewhere. You are not trying to empty your mind, which is difficult when you are worried. Shifting the focus instead of clearing the mind seems to work better for me. It has the good parts of relaxation exercises where you picture yourself in a really comfortable place, but when you're visualizing something active, it's easier to sustain.

Sheila was fortunate to be able to work with a therapist who was skilled in teaching guided imagery. This kind of assistance may be financially impossible or inaccessible for many people. While guided imagery seems simple, like riding a bicycle, there are some real skills involved. Riding a bicycle seems like a pretty simple skill that just about everybody is able to do, and you never forget once you know how to do it, but everybody knows you can't just do it right the first time; you need help in acquiring the skills to do it. There are numerous self-help books available that will help you learn guided imagery. Several of these books are included in the resources section at the back of this book.

Try the following guided imagery exercises. This one addresses a financial worry, but you can use a different worry. See how the exercise feels to you. If it helps you, great. If it doesn't seem quite right, use your creativity to redesign it so that it works for you. For instance, a walk on the beach or in a spring meadow might feel better to you. Instead of a golden light, yours might be rosy pink. You can enhance the exercise to make it longer or shorten it to fit in your time frame. Don't try to do a long exercise when you are worried about being somewhere on time or feel that you have a million other things to do.

Once you have refined the exercise to meet your needs, you may want to tape it. Play some soothing music in the background as you record your personalized guided imagery exercise. Try to do the exercise at least once a day no matter how you feel so your body learns to get into a meditative mode easily. If you get bored with this exercise, make yourself a different one. You might buy yourself a guided imagery tape. They are available at health food stores, some bookstores, and specialty shops.

Get in a comfortable sitting or lying position. Make sure you are warm enough, but not too warm, and that you will not be interrupted by the phone, doorbell, or needs of others. Stare at a spot above your head on the ceiling. Take a deep breath in to a count of eight, hold it for a count of four, let it out for a count of eight. Do that two more times.

Now close your eyes but keep them in the same position they were in when you were staring at the spot on the ceiling. Breathe in to a count of eight, hold for a count of four, out for a count of eight.

Now focus on your toes. Let them completely relax. Imagine that they are surrounded by a golden light that feels very warm and comfortable. Move the warm and comfortable feeling and the golden light through your heels and calves to your knees. Let the warm, golden light move up your thighs. Feel your whole lower body relaxing. Let the warm, golden light move very slowly through your buttocks, lower abdomen, and lower back. Feel it moving, very slowly, up your spine and through your abdomen. Feel the warm relaxation flowing into your chest and upper back. Let this golden light flow from your shoulders, down your arms, through your elbows and wrists, out through your hands and fingers. Let the golden light go slowly through your throat, up your neck, letting it all soften and relax. Let it now move up into your face. Feel the golden light of relaxation fill your jaw, cheek muscles, and around your eyes. Let it move up into your forehead. Let your whole scalp relax, feel warm and comfortable and filled with golden light. Your body is now completely relaxed, with the golden light filling every muscle and cell of your body.

Now picture yourself walking along an old country road lined with large maple trees and an ancient stone wall. It is a sunny autumn day. The leaves on the trees are shades of orange, red, and yellow. It's not too warm and not too cool. As you stroll along you feel the warmth of the sun on your back. You see a big pile of leaves by the side of the road. You lay down in the pile. The leaves envelop and cradle you. You feel safe. Everything is right with the world.

Your mind is totally focused on how good you feel. You picture yourself dealing confidently with the money situation, feeling deeply that solutions will come. As other thoughts enter your mind you wave them away, relaxing more and more deeply. You have no space for worry in this wonderful place. You feel at peace with the world. Stay in this place for a few moments.

Now, slowly wiggle your fingers and toes. Gradually return to your activities, keeping with you the wonderful feelings you enjoyed.

If you repeat this exercise, or one like it, every day, you will notice that you will feel better and better.

If you tried guided imagery, describe how it helped, or did not help, relieve your worry.

_____

_____

_____

_____

Talking about the Worry

> When I'm so involved in the problem that I can't think
> about anything else, it's time to talk it through with
> someone. Talking helps define problems and brings out
> alternatives that I might not think of on my own.

Many people find that talking about a worry helps control the worry and/or determine a course of action that might relieve the situation. People say they talk to family members, friends, and various kinds of healthcare professionals who fit the following description of a good listener:

- Pays close attention to what is being said, whether or not he or she agrees with what the person is saying

- Does not interrupt to give advice

- Only gives advice after asking the person who is talking if he or she wants feedback

- Is non-judgmental and non-critical

- Treats the person who is talking with respect

- Does not interrupt the person who is talking to get information to satisfy his or her curiosity

My study participants also had their own ideas about what makes a good listener. One man feels that a combination of supportive concern and practical suggestions, with warnings if he seems to be obsessing, helps him deal with worry. Another participant wants to be deeply listened to without the listener trying to "fix" anything for her. A different woman wants to be listened to and supported—not pitied or argued with or blown off. She wants her concerns addressed when possible.

Many of the participants agreed with the following sentiment:

> Talking about a "worry" with my spouse, a family member, or friend requires me to be able to clearly state what I'm worried about. For me that's a first step towards a solution.

Let's consider one particular worrier: She is trying to address a problem of worrying incessantly about every decision she has to make, everything that is going on in her life, every person she is close to, and even global, environmental, and social justice concerns. In order to control this worry—which has often caused her to have low energy, feel depressed, and annoy family members—she "peer counsels" regularly, at least several times a week.

Peer counseling is a structured way of talking about your problems. It provides an opportunity for unjudged, uncensored self-expression while supported by a listener. It facilitates expression of feeling, understanding of problems, discovery of helpful action, and even feeling better just from having "gotten it out." When used consistently and in a structured way, it is a free, safe, and effective self-help tool that reduces worry.

I have found that peer counseling effectively relieves worry. Talking about a worry lets me process it externally instead of letting it run around endlessly inside my head. It helps me organize my thinking and come up with a related plan of action. And listening while others work through their problems in a peer counseling setting can also be a positive process.

How to Peer Counsel

In a peer counseling session, two people spend an agreed upon amount of time together, addressing and paying attention to each other. The time is usually divided equally. For instance, if you have decided you will spend an hour together, the first half hour is focused on one person and the second half hour on the other person. It is understood that the content of these sessions is strictly confidential. Judging, criticizing, and giving advice are not allowed.

The content of the session is determined by the person who is talking. When it's your time to talk, you can use your time any way you choose. You may talk about any topic and express yourself however you need to. Don't worry if you cry, tremble, perspire, yawn, or laugh. This is you time, and you should feel comfortable enough to let your real feelings show.

The person who is listening and paying attention needs to do only that—be an attentive, supportive listener.

Here are some cautions about discussing worries with others:

It feels good to talk about it to a certain extent, but if overdone, it can cause the disturbances of worry to increase.

Sometimes I do this in lieu of action, especially whining about my weight or not exercising. I have to remember that talking with a supportive friend is helpful, but it's not going to solve my problems.

Do you have a worry that you think you might benefit from talking about?

_____ Yes

_____ No

If so, what is it? _____

Who could you talk it over with? _____

When? _____

What is your hoped for result? _____

Are you going to try peer counseling?

_____ Yes

_____ No

If so, with whom? _____

When? _____

Result of peer counseling:

_____

_____

_____

Was this the result you had hoped for?

_____ Yes

_____ No

If not, what could you do to get a better result next time?

_____

_____

_____

For more information on peer counseling, refer to the resources section at the end of the book.

Journaling

> *In my journaling, I turn the whole problem*
> *inside out. I examine every aspect of it. I write and*
> *write and write until I am totally bored with*
> *the whole thing and then I can get back to my life.*

This quote is a good description of how people feel about using journaling to control worry. The act of writing about a worry seems to help explore the worry in depth and perhaps come to some resolution about it.

All you need for journaling is some paper and a pencil or pen. Start by defining the problem in its entirety. Ask yourself the following questions to help get you started:

- What makes this worry so hard to let go of?
- Why is it such a big worry for me?
- What are the implications?
- What is the worst thing that could happen?
- What is the best thing that could happen?
- How would I like to see it resolved?
- What makes resolving it so hard?
- What are some possible solutions?
- How does the whole situation make me feel?
- What would it feel like if I didn't have this worry?
- Whose fault is it?
- What if everyone in the world had this worry?
- What's so bad about this worry?
- What could I be doing if I weren't worried about this?

Add some questions of your own.

_____

_____

_____

_____

Your answers don't have to make sense. Your writing doesn't need to be interesting. It's all right to repeat yourself over and over. Whatever is written is for you only. It's yours. You don't have to "worry" about punctuation, grammar, spelling, penmanship, neatness or staying on the lines (remember this book is about relieving worry, not adding to it). You can scribble all over the page if that makes you feel better. Don't fix your mistakes. Just keep writing. Draw or paste pictures or words in your journal if you want. Doodle. Anything goes.

Most people choose to keep their journal writings strictly confidential. The privacy of the journal should not be violated by anyone. You don't have to share your writings with anybody unless you want to. Put a note in the front of your journal that says, "This contains private information. Please do not read it without my permission. Thank you!" Some people find it helpful to share writings with family members, friends, or healthcare professionals. This is a personal choice.

If you tried journaling, describe how it helped, or did not help, relieve your worry.

_____

_____

_____

_____

Brainstorming

> *This is like being gently reminded that there*
> *is another way to look at the concern—and another way,*
> *and another way. We can live creatively—divergent*
> *thinking—or stay stuck.*

When obsessed with worry about a particular situation, "brainstorming" works well for many people. *Brainstorming* means jotting down, or speaking without thinking, a variety of different options that might provide some solution to the worry. You can do this alone or with others. For instance, if you were worried about feeling tired all the time, you might sit down with your family and brainstorm possible actions that might result in feeling less tired or more energized. Your list might include the following:

- Begin a program of daily exercise
- Schedule a physical examination
- Reduce hours at work
- Ask family members to help with household chores
- Work with a counselor on letting go of workaholic tendencies
- Eliminate junk food from my diet
- Work to lose ten pounds
- Take a daily multi-vitamin supplement
- Look at my priorities
- Ask someone to watch the kids on a regular basis
- Go to bed by 10:30 P.M. three nights in a row
- Take the train instead of driving to work

The next step is to review the list and choose one or several courses of action. Then you have to do something, that is, take some action to address the concern.

If you tried brainstorming, describe how it helped, or did not help, relieve your worry.

_____

_____

_____

_____

Action Techniques

Taking Action to Address the Concern

> *I do this all the time. It's the best thing for me to do—*
> *make a plan of attack and chip away at the problem.*
> *Sometimes I do a detailed plan, other times I'll do*
> *a spontaneous action in the moment.*

The following stories exemplify the attitude of most people in the study—taking specific action to address the concern can be an effective way to control and relieve a specific worry.

> I've found the best way to relieve worry is to do something about it. Even if it's an action that might not work, it really helps me feel better. I was worried about an upcoming visit to my in-laws. When I'm there I often feel like an outsider. So I planned several activities to take up some of the time and relieve stress during the visit—taking a walk through the neighborhood, working on my laptop computer, starting a knitting project. I knew that I might not even use these activities, that once I got there I would probably be fine. The activities felt like a safety net that relieved my worry.

In another story, a woman who had gotten past the intense grief over her husband's sudden death began to worry that she would be lonely, that she would spend the rest of her life alone. She soon realized that her worry wasn't helping the situation; in fact, family members were starting to avoid her because she spent so much time lamenting her situation. She began building a new life by volunteering at the Chamber of Commerce tourist information booth. She met a lot of new people and began to be more active socially, getting together with other volunteers for lunch and walks. She joined a women's group, which further widened her horizons. Recently she answered a personals ad and began dating.

Another woman, who was overwhelmed with worry about her son's family's move to a new community, said,

> I responded to my worry by devoting a great deal of time to being "there" for the family in transition—helping with packing, providing special experiences for my grandson, and so on. Being part of the move made me feel better about their ability to cope with the new situation.

One man said he often worries about completing projects that are a part of his job as a computer programmer.

> When I'm working on a project, I have a system for dealing with its completion. I start with the easiest thing and do the next easiest, and so on, until it is all done. So, in my mind it's all easy and no worry is involved.

Another woman's adult son called and hinted that he was bringing his large, unruly dog with him to spend the holidays at her house. After fretting about it for several days—envisioning broken ornaments, paws on the dinner table, and frightened toddlers, she wrote a letter to her son saying that she was excited to have him attend the holiday celebration, but that the dog would not be welcome, stating her reasons clearly and offering to pay ken-nel fees. Her son chose to stay home. It was not the outcome she had hoped for, but a difficult, stressful holiday for everyone would have been worse.

Another man said,

> Sometimes I catch myself worrying and realize it's secondary to my procrastination, so I just say to myself, "Just do it," instead of wor-rying about needing to do it.

One woman re-labels her "worry" as a "problem." She then addresses the problem with an action (solution) and presto, the worry is gone.

Some examples of actions mentioned by people in the study that helped to control common worries include the following:

- Saving for retirement

- Keeping at least a half tank of gas in the car at all times

- Losing weight and stopping smoking

- Having an AIDS test

- Coming "out of the closet" to eliminate worries about what others would think

- Moving to a safer location

- Calling home more often to check on the kids

Here's a word of caution from a study participant:

> Allow for multiple shots in hitting the target. Have several possible courses of action in case one or several don't work out.

Is there something you are worried about right now that might be relieved by taking action?

_____ Yes

_____ No

If so, what is the worry?

_____

What action could you take to relieve the worry?

_____

_____

_____

_____

If you tried taking action, describe how it helped, or did not help, relieve your worry.

_____

_____

_____

If you have a hard time motivating yourself to take an action to address the concern, try the following problem-solving technique.

Problem Solving

This problem-solving method really helps me. It's provided a system for creating the changes I need to make.

The problem-solving technique can be effective in directing you to the proper response to your worries. Following is an example of someone using this method.

1. **Write down one situation that is really worrying you.**

   I really want to go back to graduate school but my financial resources are very limited. I'm worried that I never will be able to go to graduate school.

2. **Make a list of possible things you can do to improve or correct the situation.**

   - *Talk to a financial aid counselor at the school about the possibility of scholarships, student loans, and/or financial aid.*
   - *Research possible scholarships in the library and on the internet.*
   - *Apply for all possible scholarships.*
   - *Apply for student loans.*
   - *Work two jobs for a year or two to earn the money.*
   - *Work and go to school at the same time, taking fewer courses and taking longer to graduate.*
   - *Go to night school and work days.*
   - *Choose a less expensive school.*

3. **Consider each idea. Which ones are not possible? Put an X next to those. Which ones would be difficult to implement? Put a question mark next to those. Which ones could you do right now? Put a Y next to those.**

   Y   *Talk to my financial aid counselor at the school about the possibility of scholarships, student loans, and/or financial aid.*
   Y   *Research possible scholarships in the library and on the internet.*
   Y   *Apply for all possible scholarships.*
   Y   *Apply for student loans.*

? *Work two jobs for a year or two to earn the money.*

? *Work and go to school at the same time, taking fewer courses and taking longer to graduate.*

? *Go to night school and work days.*

X *Choose a less expensive school. (There is no other school in this region that offers the course I need to meet my vocational goal.)*

4. **Make a contract with yourself to do all the Y things. Set specific dates.**

By Nov. 1, I will talk to my financial aid counselor at the school about the possibility of scholarships, student loans, and/or financial aid.

By Nov. 15, I will research possible scholarships in the library and on the internet.

By Dec. 15, I will apply for all possible scholarships.

By Jan. 1, I will apply for student loans.

5. **When you have completed the Y things go on to the more difficult ? things. Make a contract with yourself to do those.**

By Feb. 1, I will explore the option of working two jobs for a year or two to earn the money.

By Feb. 15, I will explore fully the option of working and going to college at the same time, taking fewer courses and taking longer to graduate.

By March 1, I will fully explore the option of going to night school and working days.

6. **Now maybe some of the X things don't look so hard. If there are any you think you could manage, make a contract and take that action.**

By April 15, if other options haven't worked out, I will explore further the option of a less expensive school.

7. **Now that you have completed these contracts, how has the situation changed?**

I am still waiting to hear about several scholarships. I have secured one. Student loans are available to cover some of my expenses. If additional scholarship money doesn't come through I have done the research and will proceed with one of the ? plans if necessary. I explored X further and I have found that there is a school in a nearby area that, although it would not be my first choice, might be an option.

Use this space to try the problem-solving technique to deal with a worry.

1. Write down a situation that is really worrying you.

---

2. Make a list of possible things you can do to improve or correct the situation. Jot them down, even if they seem overwhelming or impossible to you right now. You could ask family members and friends for ideas as well. Don't judge the ideas now. Just write them down.

_____

_____

_____

_____

_____

_____

_____

_____

_____

_____

3. Consider each idea. Which ones are not possible? Put an *X* next to those. Which ones would be difficult to implement? Put a question mark next to those. Which ones could you do right now? Put a *Y* next to those.

4. Make a contract with yourself to do all the *Y* things. Set specific dates.

By _____ (date), I will _____

By _____ , I will _____

By _____ , I will _____

By _____ , I will _____

5. When you have completed the *Y* things go on to the more difficult *?* things. Make a contract with yourself to do those.

By _____ (date), I will _____

By _____ , I will _____

By _____ , I will _____

By _____ , I will _____

6. Now maybe some of the *X* things don't look so hard. If there are any you think you could manage, make a contract and take that action.

By _____ (date), I will _____

By _____ , I will _____

By _____ , I will _____

By _____ , I will _____

7. Now that you have completed these contracts, how has the situation changed? Has the worry been satisfactorily resolved?

_____

_____

_____

_____

If the situation is still not resolved, go through this process again.

If you continue to have problems with this worry, perhaps you have some negative thought patterns or attitudes that are getting in your way. If so, and this is true of nearly everyone I've ever met, you may need to do some work on changing negative thought patterns to positive ones.

Changing Negative Thoughts, Attitudes, and Beliefs to Positive Ones

> *"Stop the tape." Don't keep trying to figure out how bad something can become. Changing negative thoughts to positive ones has helped me reduce my worry habit. It provides a structure for creating change which is helpful to me.*

Creating changes in attitudes and thought patterns can help you control your worry. Worry is often defined as obsessive negative thoughts and attitudes that are unrealistic and unproductive. Worry can become a bad habit that is not easily broken. There are ways to get rid of these negative thought patterns and attitudes. It takes hard work and persistence, as in overcoming any addictive behavior, but it's worth it.

> When a negative thought comes into my mind, I quickly "catch it" and ask myself if that serves me. Of course my answer is generally "no" and so I reframe (change) it. It has become a game at which I'm getting quite good. I no longer sit and stew in my own juices. There's too much good in life to dwell on the negatives. Actually I delight in making lemonade out of lemons!

The following quote about changing negative thinking is from the book *Conversations with God: An Uncommon Dialogue, Book 1* (Walsch 1996, 92–93).

> You say "Release all doubts, reject all fears, lose all pessimism" as if you're saying "pick me up a loaf of bread." But these things are easier said than done. "Throw all negative thoughts out of your mental constructions" might as well read "climb Mt. Everest—before lunch." It's rather a large order.

> > Harnessing your thoughts, exercising control over them, is not as difficult as it might seem. (Neither, for that matter, is climbing Mt. Everest.) It is all a matter of discipline. It is a question of intent.
> >
> > The first step is learning to monitor your thoughts; to *think about* what you are thinking about.
> >
> > When you catch yourself thinking negative thoughts—thoughts that negate your highest idea about a thing—think again! I want you to do this, *literally*. If you think you are in a doldrum, in a pickle, and no good can come of this, *think again.* If you think the world is a bad place, filled with negative events, *think again.* If you think your life is falling apart, and it looks as if you'll never get it back together again, *think again.*
> >
> > You *can* train yourself to do this. (Look how well you've trained yourself *not* to do it!)

Given those good words, try the following exercise. It's is a simple way to change negative thoughts and attitudes to positive ones.

1. Identify your negative thoughts, attitudes, or beliefs. The first step in this process is discovering your negative thoughts. They are often so much a part of you that this may be a difficult task. Get a small pad to carry with you and jot down any negative thoughts you have that increase your worry. Ask a close friend or family member if they have noticed any of your attitudes that may be negative.

Here are some examples of common negative thoughts that can increase worry:

- Something terrible is going to happen to my child (children), parents, other family members, or friends.

- I never accomplish anything.

- I never do anything right.

- Everything I do always turns out badly.

- It seems as if she (he) likes me now, but I'm sure she (he) will stop liking me when she (he) finds out what I'm really like.

- My spouse will find someone else that he or she prefers to be with.

- I'm not attractive enough to have a relationship.

- I always say the wrong thing at the wrong time.

- I'll never be able to get this done.

- I'm not good at anything.

- I'll never be able to hold down a job.

- I'll never be able to get a job doing what I really want to be doing.

- My job will end when my employer finds out I'm not really competent.

- My girlfriend (boyfriend) didn't call me tonight; she (he) must have found someone new.

- The teacher must think I'm stupid because she (he) didn't call on me when I raised my hand.

- The worst possible thing will happen every time.

- I am not as smart as my peers.

- If my parents die, it will be my fault for not going to see them as often as they would have liked.

- If I feel like something bad is going to happen, something bad will happen.

- If only my spouse would come home for dinner on time, everything would be great.

- No one will ever care about me.

- I should always dress up or people won't respect me.

- I have to do everything perfectly.

Often these negative thoughts are about future events and are not supported by present circumstances.

Use the following space to list your negative thoughts and/or attitudes that cause you worry.

_____

_____

_____

_____

_____

_____

_____

2. Check the validity of your negative thoughts, attitudes, or beliefs. The process of analyzing your negative thoughts to see if they are really true is often helpful in taking the power from these thought patterns. Choose a negative thought from the list you developed in step one of this process.

Example: *I never do anything right.*

Your negative thought: _____

    Ask yourself the following questions about the thought. Be honest with yourself. Skip over those questions that do not apply to your negative thoughts or attitudes.

Is this negative thought true?

Example: *It's not really true. I do lots of things very well, including cooking, gardening, caring for my child, and so on.*

Is your negative thought or attitude really true? Give yourself the benefit of the doubt. Provide supporting evidence.

_____

_____

_____

_____

Would a person who really cares about you be thinking this about you? If not, then should you be saying it to yourself?

Example: *No one who really cared about a person would ever think, "They can't do anything right." So I shouldn't be saying it to myself.*

_____

_____

_____

_____

Ask other people you trust if this negative thought or attitude is true.

Example: *I could ask my best friend and my spouse if "I can't do anything right" and hear their response.*

How did people you asked if your negative thought is true respond?

_____

_____

_____

_____

What do you get out of thinking your negative thought or attitude? How does it help? How does it hurt?

Example: *I don't get anything out of saying to myself, "I can't do anything right." It makes me feel terrible. It causes me to worry about things.*

_____

_____

_____

_____

Develop positive thoughts to contradict negative ones. Working with the same negative thought you worked with in the previous steps, write a positive thought that is the opposite of the negative thought.

Example: *Instead of saying, "I never do anything right," I could say, "I do lots of things right."*

Write a positive statement that is the opposite of your negative thought.

_____

_____

When developing positive thoughts, avoid using negative words such as *frightened, upset, tired, bored, not, never, can't.* Use only positive words like *happy, peaceful, loving, enthusiastic, warm.* Substitute *it would be nice if* for *should.*

Here are some examples of negative thoughts that may increase worry and positive responses:

Negative thought: *I will never feel this good again.*
Positive response: *I feel great.*

Negative thought: *I am not worth anything.*
Positive response: *I am a valuable person.*

Negative thought: *It is not okay to make mistakes.*
Positive response: *It is okay to make mistakes.*

4. Reinforce your positive thoughts. Negative thoughts have often become so familiar that change takes persistence, consistency, and creativity. Spend some time each day working on reinforcing your positive statements. You can reinforce positive responses by

- Repeating them aloud or to yourself over and over

- Writing them down over and over again, ten or twenty times

- Asking someone you trust to read your positive responses to you

- Using markers or your computer to make signs with the positive response, and hang them in obvious places around your home

- Saying "stop" to yourself and then repeating your positive response several times every time the negative thought comes up during the day

- Wearing a rubber band on your wrist and snapping it every time the negative thought comes to mind and then repeating the positive response several times.

After several weeks to several months of daily reinforcement of the positive response, you will notice that the negative thought is no longer an issue for you. If you begin to notice the negative thought again, return to your daily reinforcement activities for several more days.

After you feel that you have gotten at least one of your negative thoughts under control, go through these same exercises with other negative thoughts.

If you tried changing negative thoughts, attitudes, or beliefs, describe how it helped, or did not help, relieve your worry.

_____

_____

_____

_____

For more information about this process, refer to the resources section at the end of the book.

Other Ways to Relieve Worry

Here are a few other suggestions for relieving your worry:

- **Scheduling Worry Time**—One person said she has found it useful to schedule worry. If she feels she has some worries, she sets aside some time in the day to devote to them. Then she steadfastly refuses to worry at any other time.

- **Give the Worry Away**—Another person reported that when a situation comes up that is causing him too much worry, he imagines giving the worry to someone else. Then he imagines that the other person is doing the worrying for him.

- **Humor**—Someone else deals with worries, especially minor worries, with humor.

- **Reality Check**—One man said, "Doing a reality check with myself is critical. Is the thing I am worried about based in reality? If it is, then maybe I need to do something about it. If it isn't, then I need to let it go."

- **Analyze the Worry**—One woman shared her approach to worry. Perhaps it will help you.

Worry to me is a signal that something is wrong in my process, but not necessarily that something is wrong in my life. So I have to look at my process—like what is my fear? Will keeping that fear change what might happen? Is keeping that fear preventing me from finding the clarity that I need to make a decision? The more objectively I can look at it, the faster the worry goes away.

I take the worry and say, "What am I afraid of?" For example, "What am I afraid of in terms of quitting my job?" What's behind the fear is I won't have any money. What's behind that fear might be that I don't trust that there is something else that might provide the money. Sometimes I have to go six to ten levels down because usually the first thing you think of is not really the issue. Layer after layer after layer gets cut away. Maybe I get to the place where I say, "I don't know what I need to or want to do to get money." I tend to move from a place of not having trust to a place where I realize I already have enough money and it will come if it is needed.

4

Focusing Your
Attention Away
from Worry

*When my thinking goes in circles with no
new thought or ideas, then it's time to let it
rest and hope new inspiration comes along.*

Sometimes it may feel better to focus on something else or on nothing at all
than to try to deal with the worry at hand. Or perhaps you have an unde-
fined, overall worried feeling and don't quite know what to do with it. The
following meditation/stress reduction and relaxation techniques will help
you take your mind off your worries. They include focusing on detail, progressive relaxation, prayer, and breathing techniques. Other techniques
addressed in this chapter are diversionary activities, exercise, affirmations,
and helping others.

Meditation/Stress Reduction and Relaxation Techniques

*If I get too absorbed in a problem and find
that intense worry is wasting my time,
I will often choose to meditate. How long I
meditate is usually determined by how busy I am.*

Responses from people in the study who have tried to use meditation to reduce worry range from very enthusiastic to very negative. Those people who reported that they considered themselves worried people (that is, worry is a state of being for them more than it is related to specific concerns) found meditation to be especially useful. The positive responses and my own experience with the regular practice of meditation, stress reduction, and/or relaxation techniques have led me to believe that this is an avenue of relief that should be explored by anyone who wants to relieve a worry habit.

Here's a simple way to meditate: Sit in your favorite chair. Close your eyes and just notice your breathing. Try to clear your head by waving the thoughts by as they come into your mind. This isn't always easy to do. When you notice a new thought has crept in, acknowledge the thought, let it go, and return your attention to your breathing. On your next inhalation, count fifty. As you exhale, count forty-nine. Inhale—forty-eight, exhale—forty-seven. Continue on down to zero, letting go of any thoughts that may pass through your mind. When you get to zero, you can remain in that relaxed state for as long as you like. When you resume your activities, you should find, as I often do, that the worry has diminished dramatically.

Many people didn't feel they could use meditation stress reduction and relaxation techniques to relieve worry because they

- Didn't know how

- Couldn't take the time to do it on a regular basis (regular practice seems essential to effective use of these techniques)

- Couldn't take the time to do it when worry becomes problematic

- Didn't think they were able to achieve a meditative or relaxed state

The best way to address all of these concerns is to participate in a meditation stress reduction and relaxation course or workshop. Many hospitals and mental health centers offer them free of charge or for a small fee. Healing centers and healthcare practitioners of various kinds also offer this kind of training. Once you've learned these techniques in a structured, comfortable setting and have experienced the benefits, using them regularly becomes a higher priority and is easier to do.

A person who is very enthusiastic about meditation as a way to relieve worry said,

> I have benefited from guided meditation in groups. One of my earliest experiences with meditation was in a group workshop. I was teaching a course in a seminary plus doing my normal work—and feeling exhausted. I attended a six-session "Spiritual Transformation" workshop. For several sessions nothing happened. Then one evening we did an unusual exercise and at the close of the evening I was in an entirely different mental, psychological, and spiritual place. It was amazing and wonderful. Over the years since then I have practiced meditation before getting out of bed and at any time during the day.

Another enthusiastic response was,

> Plain old sitting quietly and "tuning in" has worked well for me and is important to do daily.

One woman said whenever she finds herself worrying too much she briefly stops whatever she is doing and breathes slowly, blocking out her thoughts, relaxing.

Massage/body work helps another woman to relieve worry. She said,

> It works for the time I'm getting the massage and brings my worry down a notch afterward.

Following are several examples of simple meditation stress reduction and relaxation techniques that may help you reduce worry.

Focusing on Detail

One simple but effective meditative technique is to stare for ten minutes at a lovely, detailed card or picture. I keep a stack of cards I have received handy for just this purpose.

Set a timer for ten minutes. Sit in a comfortable, quiet spot. Then stare at the picture, closely examining every detail, for at least ten minutes. Focusing on detail is simple, safe, refreshing, and often very helpful in getting relief from worry.

Being Present in the Moment

Most of the worry in your life comes from thinking about the past or worrying about the future. When all of your attention is focused in the present moment, or on what you are doing right now, there is no room to feel anything else. When meditating, all of your attention is focused on the present moment. When other thoughts intrude you just turn your awareness back to the present. It is not necessary to be alone in a special place to focus all your attention on the moment. Try doing it when you are feeling irritated waiting in a line, stopped at a street light, stuck in traffic, feeling overwhelmed or worried. Notice how this makes you feel.

Progressive Muscle Relaxation

This exercise is very popular for achieving a meditative state and reducing worry. It can be modified to meet individual needs. I often use it to put myself to sleep when worries are overwhelming me at bedtime. While an audiotape for guidance through this exercise can be helpful, it is not necessary. If you make a tape of this for yourself, be sure you leave enough time (ten to fifteen seconds) to tense and relax your muscles. However, the simplicity of this exercise makes it easy to learn and go through in your mind when using a tape is not possible.

The purpose of this technique is to get you to focus on body sensations and how relaxation feels by systematically tensing and then relaxing specific muscle groups. In the process you forget about your worries and end up feeling just great or sleeping soundly.

Find a quiet space where you will not be disturbed. You can do it either lying on your back or sitting in a chair, as long as you are comfortable.

Begin by closing your eyes gently. Clench your right fist as tightly as you can. Be aware of the tension as you do so. Keep it clenched for a few seconds. Relax. Feel the looseness in your right hand and compare it to the tension you felt previously. Tense your right fist again, relax it, and again, notice the difference.

Clench your left fist as tightly as you can. Be aware of the tension as you do so. Keep it clenched for a few seconds. Relax. Feel the looseness in your left hand and compare it to the tension you felt previously. Tense your left fist again, relax it, and again, notice the difference.

Bend your elbows and tense your biceps as hard as you can. Notice the feeling of tightness. Keep them tensed for a few seconds. Relax and straighten out your arms. Let the relaxation flow through your arms and compare it to the tightness you felt previously. Tense and relax your biceps again.

Wrinkle your forehead as tightly as you can. Feel the tension as you hold this position for a few seconds. Relax and let your forehead smooth out. Feel your forehead and scalp becoming relaxed. Frown for a few seconds and notice the tension spreading through your forehead again. Relax and allow your forehead to become smooth.

Close your eyes very tightly for a few seconds. Feel the tension. Relax your eyes. Tense and relax your eyes again. Let them remain gently closed.

Clench your jaw for a few seconds and feel the tension. Relax your jaw, with your lips slightly parted. Notice the difference. Clench and relax again.

Press your tongue against the roof of your mouth. Hold it there for a few seconds. Relax. Do this again.

Press and purse your lips together for a few seconds. Relax them. Repeat this.

Feel the relaxation throughout your arms, forehead, scalp, eyes, jaw, tongue, and lips.

If you are sitting in a chair, hold your head back as far as it can comfortably go and observe the tightness in your neck. Hold this position for a few seconds. Roll your head to the right and notice how the tension moves and changes. Hold this position for a few seconds. Roll your head to the left and notice how the tension moves and changes. Hold this position for a few seconds. Straighten your head and bring it forward, pressing your chin towards your chest. Notice the tension in your throat and the back of your neck. Hold this position for a few seconds. Relax and allow your head, neck, and shoulders to return to a comfortable position. Allow yourself to feel more and more relaxed. Shrug your shoulders up towards your ears. Hold this position for a few seconds. Relax your shoulders. Allow them to drop back and feel the relaxation moving through your neck, throat, and shoulders. Feel the lovely, very deep relaxation.

Give your whole body a chance to relax. Feel how comfortable and heavy you are.

Breathe in and fill your lungs completely. Hold your breath for a few seconds and notice the tension. Let your breath out and let your chest become loose. Continue relaxing, breathing gently in and out. Repeat this breathing several times and notice the tension draining out of your body.

Tighten your stomach and hold the tightness for a few seconds. Feel the tension. Relax your stomach. Place your hand on your stomach. Breathe deeply into your stomach, pushing your hand up. Hold for a few seconds and then relax. Arch your back, without straining, keeping the rest of your body as relaxed as possible. Hold this position for a few seconds. Notice the tension in your lower back. Relax deeper and deeper.

Tighten your buttocks and thighs. Hold this position for a few seconds. Relax and notice the difference. Do this again. Curl your toes down, making your calves tense. Hold this position for a few seconds. Notice the tension. Relax. Bend your toes towards your face, creating tension in your shins. Relax and notice the difference.

Feel the heaviness throughout your lower body as the relaxation gets deeper and deeper. Relax your feet, ankles, calves, shins, knees, thighs, and buttocks. Let the relaxation spread to your stomach, lower back, and chest. Let go more and more. Experience deeper and deeper relaxation in your shoulders, arms, and hands, deeper and deeper. Notice the feeling of looseness and relaxation in your neck, jaws, and all your facial muscles. Just relax and be aware of how your whole body feels before you return to your other activities.

Prayer

A number of people in the study said that when worries overwhelm them, they meditate in the form of praying or reaching out to a spiritual source. They felt comforted and supported through prayer. Some described it as a process of turning the worry over to their spiritual support and then forgetting about or letting go of the worry. Others said they asked for guidance in dealing with the worry or letting go of it. One person said,

> I use prayer every morning to think about concerns in my life and have a standard group of thoughts. This works wonders for me.

Another said,

> I have had many times when a problem laid at God's feet has provided an answer—not immediately, but eventually, and not the necessarily hoped for or expected—but an answer.

Breathing Techniques

Specific breathing techniques have been helpful to those who are trying to relieve worry. They can be used safely by anyone, anywhere. When you focusing on breathing or making changes in the way you breathe, it's very hard to worry.

Some breathing techniques are very simple. For instance one person finds it very calming to just say "in" as she breathes in and "out" as she breathes out when she finds herself in stressful situations and is worrying excessively. Another woman said that when she finds herself worrying, or as she calls it "fretting," she reminds herself to breathe deeply and focus on a cloud, tree, or some other natural object.

A breathing technique that I call a "square breath" has helped my feelings change from very stressed and worried to calm and relaxed. Breathe in deeply to a count of eight, noticing your lungs and diaphragm filling with air. Then hold your breath for a count of eight and exhale for a count of eight. Then rest to a count of eight before you take another breath. Repeat this over and over until you feel relaxed and calm. You may feel a bit light-headed but that feeling passes quickly. After I have done several square breaths, my worries don't seem as significant or they have vanished altogether.

You may want to try the following breathing exercises when you are having a hard time with worry.

Breathing Awareness

Lie down on the floor with your legs flat or bent at the knees, your arms at your sides, palms up, and your eyes closed. Take a deep breath through your nose if you can. If you can't breathe through your nose, breathe through your mouth. Focus on your breathing. Continue to breathe deeply. Place your hand on the place that seems to rise and fall the most as you breathe. If this place is on your chest, practice breathing more deeply so that your abdomen rises and falls most noticeably. (When you are nervous or anxious you tend to breathe short, shallow breaths in the upper chest.) Now place both hands on your abdomen and notice how your abdomen rises and falls with each breath. Notice if your chest is moving in harmony with your abdomen. Continue to do this for several minutes. Get up slowly. This is something you can do during a break at school or work. If you can't lay down you can do it sitting in a chair.

Deep Breathing

This exercise can be practiced in a variety of positions. However, it is most effective if you can do it lying down with your knees bent and your spine straight. After lying down, scan your body with your mind, searching out places that feel tense. Place one hand on your abdomen and one hand on your chest. Inhale slowly and deeply through your nose into your abdomen to push up your hand as much as feels comfortable. Your chest should only move a little in response to the movement in your abdomen. Repeat several of these breaths. When you feel at ease with your breathing, inhale through your nose and exhale through your mouth, making a relaxing whooshing sound as you gently blow out. This will relax your mouth, tongue, and jaw. Continue taking long, slow, deep breaths that raise and lower your abdomen. As you become more and more relaxed, focus on the sound and feeling of your breathing. Continue this deep breathing for five or ten minutes at a time, once or twice a day, or when you are feeling stressed from worry. At the end of each session, scan your body for tension. As you become used to this exercise, you can practice it in a standing, sitting, or lying position wherever you happen to be. Use this exercise whenever you feel very worried.

Transformational Breathing

Because several study participants used specific breathing techniques to relieve worry, I interviewed a skilled breathing facilitator, Bev White, for more information. She said,

> In general, taking deep breaths relieves worry for people because when they worry they unconsciously hold their breath as a way of trying to control their feelings. Consciously taking deep breaths is a way to reverse the suppression of the feeling. It also has a physical aspect to it. Worry creates muscular tension and prevents oxygen

from reaching all the cells. Often when people breathe deeply, that physical tension relaxes and oxygen can get to the whole body. Breathing can allow a person to let go of what they are feeling. It's a freeing energy.

I teach Transformational Breathing. It is an hour of conscious breathing. When people are interested in this special breathing technique, they go to see a qualified breathing facilitator so they can experience the benefits and be guided through the process. Many people report that, at the end of the session, they have reached clarity about something that was a concern in their life. Sometimes the clarity comes around an issue they needed to make a decision about. The worry was able to be released because they clearly saw what their decision needed to be and that was okay. If the person could get to the place where they accepted that they couldn't do anything about a situation, then they could let the worry go as well.

If you are going to get into breath work, you really have to want to be a participant in creating change in yourself. Not only is this kind of breathing participatory, you see change much more quickly. By teaching people breathing techniques, they become empowered to embark on a journey of self-healing.

To get more information on specific breathing techniques and for referral to a breathing facilitator, ask local alternative healthcare providers, or check with an alternative medical services resource referral guide or with healing centers. A search on the internet under "breathing" will reveal a multitude of helpful resources.

Bev recommends the following breathing exercises, which were adapted from a write-up from the Transformational Breath Foundation and are available to be passed on to anyone.

Balancing Breath for Centering Self

If you're right-handed, place the thumb of your right hand over your right nostril and inhale through your left nostril to the count of eight. Hold the breath for a count of eight. Cover your left nostril with the index finger of the right hand and exhale through your right nostril to a count of eight and hold the breath for a count of eight. Cover your right nostril with the thumb and repeat the cycle ten times.

Hong Sah Breath for Calming the Mind

Inhale slowly through your nose while mentally repeating the word "Hong" as you inhale. Hold the breath for a count of 10. Then exhale slowly through the mouth as you say the word "Sah" out loud. Repeat a few times.

If you tried meditation/stress reduction and relaxation techniques to relieve worry, describe which one you tried and how they helped, or did not help, relieve your worry.

_____

_____

_____

_____

Refer to the resources section at the end of the book for more information on these techniques.

Diversionary Activities

I use diversionary activities a lot.
Using more brain cells to do or think
differently leaves little space for bothersome things.

When worry becomes overwhelming, many people find it helpful to divert their attention by getting involved in some activity they really enjoy. Here are some quotes from people in the study about diversionary activities:

I have tried a lot of diversions—the effectiveness varies depending on how worried I am and what it's about. Generally, diversion is only effective for short-term concerns, until the situation is resolved.

Diversionary activities are imperative or I lose perspective.

Recently I was worried about my daughter having to move when she didn't want to. It was hard for me to see her and her six-year-old in pain. I was glad to be so busy with my community work during times when I couldn't be helpful.

Getting involved and thinking about something else always helps me relieve worry.

When going in circles—I like to watch TV, read a good book, and be with people.

Playing tennis, running, swimming, walking in the woods and gardening help me to refocus my thoughts and reduce my worry.

If I am obsessing on a problem or worry, I find that it helps to take on small tasks or projects to take my mind off the worry and give me a sense of accomplishment.

I take a walk on the beach and simply meander along the water observing the movement of the tides and what is happening on the beach. There have been times when I wander through a nearby cemetery. These diversionary activities work for me. The time, the place, the concern determine which one may or may not be effective.

I make a list and start at the top, checking off activities as I complete them—exercise, work in the garden, pick flowers, sit beside garden, canoe, walk the dog, call an old friend, go to a movie, go out to dinner. This really works for me.

Of course, diversionary activities may not work for everyone. One person said,

I try to reduce worry by using diversionary activities, but it makes things worse because I'm not dealing with the situation that is worrying me.

If you think diversionary activities might help reduce your worries, list specific activities that you might try. Use the following list to help you think of activities you enjoy. Check off those that you want to put on your list. Or add activities that interest you that aren't on this list.

_____ Journaling

_____ Listening to music

_____ Making music

_____ Building models

_____ Cooking

_____ Photography

_____ Gardening

_____ Exercising

_____ Needlework

Diversionary activities I could use to reduce worry:

_____   _____

_____   _____

_____   _____

_____   _____

———————————————   ———————————————

———————————————   ———————————————

Keep a copy of this list in a handy place so you can refer to it when you need to. When you are worrying excessively, take the time to engage yourself in one of these activities. The hardest thing about using diversionary activities to reduce worry is breaking away from the worry and getting started on an activity. It gets easier the more you do it. It's replacing a bad habit with something that will make you feel better.

If you tried diversionary activities, describe which ones and how they helped, or did not help, relieve your worry.

———————————————————————————————————————

———————————————————————————————————————

———————————————————————————————————————

———————————————————————————————————————

Exercise

> *I think being fit certainly helps us process*
> *our life stuff. Maybe it has something*
> *to do with having good circulation.*

Exercise helps reduce worry in many different ways. When you exercise, you may notice that

- You feel better (physically and emotionally)

- You sleep better

- Your memory and ability to concentrate improve

- You feel less irritable and anxious

- Your self-esteem increases

It is often difficult to motivate yourself to exercise, especially when you are worried or have a lot on your mind. Remember, though, even a few minutes of moving will help. Do the best you can. If you can't do it at all right now, don't give yourself a hard time. Listening to music may provide motivation.

Do whatever it is you enjoy! People in the study noted the following kinds of exercise:

- Walking

- Running

- Swimming

- Skating (ice skating, inline skating)

- Hiking

- Skateboarding

- Surfing

- Skiing

- Dancing

- Yoga

- Outdoor chores, such as cutting wood, raking, gardening

- Playing with your pet

One man said that, aside from sleep and good solid food, exercise is his best medicine.

> I get vigorous exercise three to five times a week in addition to easy walks in my daily routine.

Another person shares a word of warning:

> I try to get in more walking and dancing, but sometimes getting enough becomes, itself, a source of worry.

If you haven't exercised recently or have health problems that may affect your ability to exercise, check with your physician before beginning an exercise program.

_____ I exercise and I feel it helps focus my attention away from my worries.

_____ I exercise but I don't feel that it helps focus my attention away from my worries.

_____ I am going to start exercising to help focus my attention away from my worries. I am going to try (kind of exercise) _____ .

If you tried exercise, describe how it helped, or did not help, relieve your worry.

_____

_____

_____

_____

Other Ideas

There were a number of ideas for relieving worry that were mentioned just once or several times in the study, but nevertheless seem worthy of mention. Perhaps one or several of them will feel right to you.

Affirmations

Affirmations are positive statements that can be repeated over and over when a worry comes up. Here are some examples:

- Everything will be okay.

- I've done it before, I can do it again.

- Others have gotten through this and I will too.

- I have all the skills I need to get this done.

- Focus on positive thoughts.

- I'm a great person with a lot of ability.

- I can solve this problem.

A woman in the study said,

Sometimes affirmations help a lot. It's as close as I come to prayer.

If you tried using affirmations, describe how it helped, or did not help, relieve your worry.

_____

_____

_____

_____

List several affirmations that you feel might be helpful.

_____

_____

_____

Help Others

Go out and do something for someone else. The positive feeling you can get from helping others just might take your mind off of your worries. You can do something for someone close to you—a family member or a friend. Some examples of helpful activities include:

- Take their dog for a walk

- Entertain their children

- Do a household chore

- Rake leaves

- Mow the grass

- Plant some flowers

- Cook them a meal or bake them a loaf of bread

- Chat with an elderly or lonely person in your neighborhood.

Helping people you don't know can also effectively relieve worry. You can be a onetime or regular volunteer for a community organization. You don't have to make a commitment to volunteer on a regular basis; every single action will help both you and someone else. You can even do something nice for someone you don't know on the spur of the moment.

For ideas of where to volunteer, call your local volunteer center or a senior volunteer program.

If you tried helping others, describe how it helped, or did not help, relieve your worry.

_____

_____

_____

_____

5

Other Considerations in Solving Your Worry Problem

I seemed to be worried all the time and, no matter what I tried, I couldn't seem to get a handle on it.

It may be that you have searched and searched for ways to control your worry. You have tried technique after technique, given each of them a fair trial, and nothing seemed to work. Before you give up and say, "I guess I'm just always going to have to live with this worry problem," it might be beneficial to think about your overall health and well-being and look into some so-called alternative options that may provide some relief.

Your Overall Health

People in the study said that when they feel like they are generally in poor health, their worry about everything increases. While this may seem like an indirect route to controlling worry, it may be time to consider the following questions and take some action. Relief may be just around the corner.

Are You in Good Physical and Emotional Health?

If your excessive worry is accompanied by some of the following symptoms or a generalized feeling of poor health, you need a complete physical examination to see if some kind of medical or emotional condition is a factor:

- Fatigue

- Feelings of listlessness

- Chronic diffuse pain

- Dry skin

- Difficulty losing weight

- Not hungry or hungry all the time

- Generalized anxiety

Some of the most common ailments that can cause worry are

- Hypothyroidism: The thyroid gland keeps all the bodily functions humming along. If it's not working up to par, you won't feel well and you will worry more. This is easily corrected by taking supplemental thyroxin.

- Hypoglycemia: This is more commonly known as low blood sugar and is easily corrected through diet.

- Chronic fatigue syndrome: A difficult-to-treat condition that can keep you from doing the things you want to do. There is no "one size fits all" treatment. Relief comes from a persistent search to find the right answer for you.

- Fibromyalgia: While this painful, debilitating condition is difficult to diagnose and treat, it can be effectively managed to achieve long-term wellness and relief from resulting worry.

- Diagnosable disorders: Excessive worry may indicate that you have a treatable disorder. If you feel that your worry is significant enough to suggest that you have an anxiety or mood disorder, consult your physician or a therapist. He or she will be able to give you a proper diagnosis and suggest a course of action. Bring this book in; it can be a valuable tool for work with a therapist.

If you think your worry may be difficult to control due to an ailment or diagnosable disorder, what actions would you like to take to improve your health and relieve your worry?

_____

_____

_____

For more information, refer to chapter 13, "Health Issues," and the resources section at the end of the book.

Are You Eating Well?

Take the following quiz to find out about your eating habits.

1. Does your diet consist of mostly processed food—canned, frozen, ready-made, or fast foods?

_____ Yes

_____ No

2. Are the foods you eat high in processed flours, fat, sugar, salt, and additives?

_____ Yes

_____ No

3. Do you drink more than two cups of coffee (or use other forms of caffeine) daily?

_____ Yes

_____ No

4. Do you usually eat on the run instead of sitting down to enjoy your meal?

_____ Yes

_____ No

5. Do you often feel bloated, gaseous, and/or very sleepy after you eat?

_____ Yes

_____ No

6. Do you often feel stuffed after you eat?

_____ Yes

_____ No

7. Has your physician told you (or do you already know) that you need to gain or lose weight?

    ____ Yes

    ____ No

8. Is your diet high in fresh vegetables and fruits?

    ____ Yes

    ____ No

If you answered yes to any of the first seven questions and no to the eighth question, your diet may be causing you to feel lousy. When people don't feel healthy, they report that they worry more—and not just about feeling lousy, but about everything.

Taking better care of yourself by controlling your diet, will help you increase your overall sense of well-being and decrease your overall worry. While determining what kind of diet is best for you is a decision you need to make for yourself—perhaps in consultation with your physician or, even better, a nutritionist or a naturopathic physician—there are some general guidelines that you can try right away.

- Add wholesome, natural, and fresh foods to your diet as much as possible. Health food stores, food cooperatives, farmers' markets, and some supermarkets are good sources of fresh, organic foods. While it may seem that these foods are more expensive, when you choose them instead of junk foods, the increase in your food bill will be hardly noticeable. Eat at least three to five servings of vegetables each day along with two to four servings of fresh fruit.

- Avoid those foods that are high in processed flours, fat, sugar, salt, and food additives. Read the labels. If sugar is a main ingredient, along with processed flours, salt, and a lot of words you can't pronounce, put it back on the shelf.

- If you often feel gaseous, bloated, or very sleepy after you eat, you may benefit from cutting down on sugar in your diet. The amount of sugar we eat in our society has increased substantially in the last century. Years ago a sugary snack was a very special treat. Now we find sugar added to almost everything we eat. Our bodies don't know what to do with it.

- Reduce your intake of coffee, other caffeinated beverages, and chocolate (caffeine is known to cause anxiety and its close cousin—worry). Don't cut down on caffeine all at once. Reduce it slowly or you will develop flu-like symptoms and be quite grouchy.

- Have a rule for yourself that you will always be sitting down at the table when you are eating. Put on some quiet music and light some candles. If you live with others, tell them you are trying to have calmer mealtimes and work with them to develop a rule that prohibits arguing or discussion of loaded topics at mealtime. At times you may want to refrain from answering the phone at mealtimes, too.

- Eat only as much food as you need to feel satisfied. Don't stuff yourself. Make it a habit to eat three healthy meals a day with several healthy between-meal snacks if desired. Don't skip any meals.

- If you are often too tired to cook after a busy day, or nothing in the house appeals to you, do some thoughtful grocery shopping. Buy a supply of healthy foods that you enjoy. Include foods that are easy to prepare. There are some healthy frozen dinners that you can have on hand for those days when you are exhausted.

- There are many excellent resource books, cookbooks, and magazines that can help you learn more about good nutrition and guide you in changing your food habits. Most libraries have a section of books that deal with food and nutrition. It helps enormously in changing eating habits to have recipes that you really like; alternatively, don't make yourself eat foods you don't care for or you will quickly abandon the new diet, but do challenge yourself to try new foods.

- Set reasonable goals for creating changes in eating habits. Reward yourself with a non-food treat each time you reach a goal. It might be a flower, a book or tape you have been wanting, an article of clothing, seeing a movie, taking time off from other responsibilities or giving yourself $5 to spend in a thrift store.

If you feel that changing your eating habits will increase your sense of well-being and helps you control your worry, list three dietary changes you'd like to make and set a goal for when you'd like to implement each change.

Change: _____ When: _____

Change: _____ When: _____

Change: _____ When: _____

Are You Getting Enough Exercise?

If you are dealing with a case of "couch potato fever," beginning an exercise routine is guaranteed to help you feel better and reduce the worry in your life. It's hard to worry when you are walking in the woods, running through the park, ice skating, skiing, or bicycling. In addition, the exercise will improve your overall health. If you are older, out of shape, or have a health condition, check with your doctor before increasing your level of exercise.

Exercise options continue to increase. Almost everyone can find an activity that suits them. You could go to the gym or lift weights at home. You could swim in a pool at the YMCA or hike in the back country. The trick is to find something that appeals to you. Consider the following options and put a check mark next to the ones that interest you:

_____	Swimming	_____	Walking
_____	Skating	_____	Skiing
_____	Hiking	_____	Running
_____	Lifting weights	_____	Bicycling
_____	Yoga	_____	Aerobics
_____	Shooting hoops	_____	Gardening
_____	Shoveling snow	_____	Mowing the lawn
_____	Splitting and stacking wood	_____	Raking leaves
_____	Competitive sports (basketball, baseball, soccer)		

What other kinds of exercise would you like to try?

_____

_____

Do you think you would feel better if you got more exercise?

_____ Yes

_____ No

If you do, what are you going to do?	When are you going to do it?	How often?
_____	_____	_____
_____	_____	_____
_____	_____	_____
_____	_____	_____
_____	_____	_____

You may want to give yourself a treat after you have exercised a certain number of times. It could be something specific to the activity, like a pair of running shoes or a new walking outfit. It could also be something totally unrelated, like a tool for your workshop or a pretty scarf. Putting it in writing may help you stick to your goal.

After I have exercised (how often and how long) _____ *for at least* (days, weeks) _____ *I am going to treat myself with the following:*

Are You Getting Enough Light through Your Eyes?

> *The worst time of year for me used to be around the holidays. I spent more time in "useless worry" than at any other time of the year. I used to think it was related to "holiday nostalgia," but since I have increased my exposure to outdoor light, my worries seem to have vanished.*

In recent years the connection between lack of light through the eyes and depressed feelings has been confirmed. Many people notice that as the hours of daylight shorten in the fall and winter, they feel worse and worse. This depressed mood is called seasonal affective disorder, or SAD. If you have SAD your sense of overall well-being will diminish and your worries will increase as the days get shorter. You may notice the same phenomena when there is a series of cloudy days. If you have noticed this, don't *worry*; that won't help. But the following suggestions will:

- Check with your physician about possible treatments. If your physician does not have the necessary expertise, ask for a referral to a doctor who is knowledgeable about light therapy.

- Spend as much time outside as possible, getting out even if you can only do it for a half hour during your lunch break and even on cloudy days.

- Have your indoor working space situated as closely as possible to windows or other sources of outside light.

- Keep indoor spaces well lit.

Even when you are exposing yourself to light, you must remember to **never look directly into the sun.**

If you think that SAD may be part or all of the reason you worry so much in the fall and winter months, what are you going to do about it?

_____

_____

_____

_____

Alternative Remedies

Vitamins, Minerals, Herbs, or Other Food Supplements

> *I definitely notice my worry level goes*
> *up when I forget to use the food supplements*
> *that I've found make me feel better.*

Vitamins, minerals, herbs, amino acids, and other food supplements have been used successfully by study participants to relieve feelings of worry and to enhance an overall sense of well-being.

The optimum way to find out which of these products would be helpful and safe for you to use is through consultation with a healthcare professional, such as a naturopathic physician, who has extensive training and experience in this area. However, the cost of such a consultation may be prohibitive for many people. In fact, dealing with the added expense of such a consultation may add to an already long list of worries. Some healthcare plans are now providing coverage for these services, but this is the exception rather than the rule. Only by letting our elected officials know that these services should be covered, and that they often prevent more costly healthcare, will this picture change.

If you can't afford a consultation, there are many excellent reference books and resources available that can help you decide which of these products would be good options for you. Most health food stores have an extensive section of literature that can provide you with the guidance you need. Check out the qualifications of the authors before buying a book. Store personnel can also be a source of useful information. *Prescription for Nutritional Healing: A Practical A–Z reference to Drug-Free Remedies Using Vitamins, Minerals, Herbs, and Food Supplements* by J. Balch and P. Balch is an outstanding guide.

I find these substances invaluable when I'm experiencing obsessive worries. I also have a food supplement regimen I follow daily that helps keep me going. I know that if I neglect this regime for several days, my mood goes down and my worries increase.

If you are going to try food supplements, keep the following in mind.

- Never use more than the recommended dosages.

- Carefully monitor how you are feeling when you are using these supplements.

- Discontinue their use if you notice unusual side effects.

If you have ever tried using supplements to relieve worry, describe what you used and how it helped, or did not help, relieve your worry.

Homeopathic Remedies

When I'm obsessively worried, often several
doses of what seems like a benign homeopathic
remedy is just what I need to take the edge off.

The science of homeopathy is based on the premise that the body has the ability to heal itself. Homeopathic study has documented thousands of substances that, when taken in a highly diluted dose of the original substance, can cure the symptoms you would get if you took a large dose of the same substance. For instance—allium is from onions. If you cut onions it will make you teary. If you have a runny nose and are teary, a tiny amount of allium will reduce these symptoms.

Homeopathic medications are quite safe and relatively inexpensive. If one remedy doesn't work, you can give another a try. You can also use several different homeopathic remedies at the same time. These remedies are available in many health food stores. The label will often describe the symptoms that may be relieved by taking the remedy, along with the suggested dose.

I have used a homeopathic remedy called *ignatia amara* when I have worries about family matters. I notice gradual and subtle relief. If I've been treated rudely by a friend or co-worker, *natrum mur* helps me get rid of the obsessive worry—"What did I do wrong?"—that generally accompanies such an incident. *Staphysagria* and *nux vomica* are particularly effective for obsessive worries. Others that may be tried include *chamomilla, colocynthis, gelsemium, argentum nitricum,* and *lycopodium*. Several people in the study said that they use a Bach Flower remedy called Rescue Remedy to relieve worry.

If homeopathic medications sound like an intriguing way for you to help relieve your worry, consult a homeopathic physician, purchase a book on homeopathy, or look it up on the internet. There are several books on homeopathy listed in the resources section at the back of this book.

If you have tried using homeopathic medications to relieve worry, describe what you used and how it helped, or did not help, relieve your worry.

_____

_____

_____

Aromatherapy

*Aromatherapy helps relieve worry. Scents like lavender
or orange blossom or sage are quite soothing.*

While scents may seem like an unusual way to relieve worry, the effects of particular smells on how you feel cannot be discounted. An aromatherapist I know, Beverly White, said,

> To use aromas to let go of a worry habit you would have to decide how you want to approach worry. If, when you relieve the worry, you want to feel euphoric or uplifted, try jasmine, rose, and clary sage. In addition, all the citrus fragrances are uplifting when you are feeling down. If you just want to relax and let your worries drift away, try lavender, orange blossom, sandalwood, and chamomile.
>
> Balancing fragrances like bergamot, frankincense, geranium, rose, and rosewood are very specific to relieving worry. They tend to regulate highs and lows, address fear and anxiety.
>
> The stimulating fragrances like tea tree, rosemary, eucalyptus, and peppermint tend to make you worry more, but don't rule them out if you are drawn to them because, if you just love an aroma, it can also have a therapeutic effect on you.
>
> There are also some blended scents that will really help relieve worry. If you are not sure which one is right for you, find the one that you love to smell and it will make you feel great.

Usually places that sell natural fragrances, like health food stores, health spas, and natural pharmacies, have a tester rack so you can find the scent that is right for you. Scents come in a variety of forms including room scenters, perfume oils, lotions, body oil blends, bath products, hair products, candles, and foot scrubbers. Most people find the natural fragrances preferable to synthetic.

An essential oil is a pure, undiluted fragrance and should not be used directly on skin unless it is tea tree or lavender. Add essential oil to a vegetable oil to make body oil, add it to an unscented body lotion, or put it in water in an aroma burner. You can add it to distilled water and spray it around the room or on yourself. A few drops can be put directly in bath water as you are running it.

The best way to learn about aromatherapy is to check out a good resource book or consult with an aromatherapy specialist. Don't necessarily take the word of a shop owner who is anxious to sell a product. It's an individual therapy; you have to choose a scent that fits you.

If you have tried aromatherapy to relieve worry, describe what scent(s) you used and how it helped, or did not help, relieve your worry.

_____

_____

_____

Using Your Senses

There are other senses, in addition to smell, that, given appropriate attention, can help to relieve worry.

Sight

Color can help you feel better and relieve worry. This became clear to me when I had a negative response to color. I spent two hours in a room in which one wall was painted a dark pea green and the others were painted a shade of yellow that looked terrible with the pea green. I found that I was tense and worried the whole time I was there. I usually feel much better when I'm in a room painted in some light pastel or rosy color. I kept this in mind when choosing the colors to redecorate my new home. Many of my friends have commented on how "great" the colors make them feel.

Following are some ideas to give color a more important place in your life and help relieve worries when you don't feel great. Which ideas appeal to you?

_____ Choose clothing in your favorite colors.

_____ Do some redecorating with colors you enjoy. If cost is an issue, check out your local thrift store for colorful curtains and spreads.

_____ Adorn your walls with pictures in colors you enjoy.

_____ Have fresh flowers in your living space as often as possible.

Hearing

Pay attention to your sense of hearing by pampering yourself with delightful music you really enjoy. Your worries will float away. Find a good music store where you can listen to music before you purchase it. Then collect tapes or compact discs. Libraries often have records and tapes available for loan. If you enjoy music, make it an essential part of every day.

Touch

Help yourself feel even more cool, calm, and collected by giving your skin a treat. Have a massage by a skilled professional, give yourself a massage, or ask your spouse or a good friend to give you a massage. Enhance your sense of well-being by wearing something soft and cuddly that feels really good.

If you have tried appealing to your senses of sight, hearing, and touch to control worry, describe what you used and how it helped, or did not help, relieve your worry.

_____

_____

_____

Your Ideas

Have you discovered any other ways to reduce generalized worry? What are they and how well do they work?

Strategy to Reduce Generalized Worry	How Well Did It Work?
_____	_____
_____	_____
_____	_____
_____	_____
_____	_____

6

Reducing the
Possibility of Worry

*In my case, if I were a good planner, more than half of
the things I worry about would disappear.*

While most people agree that it is not possible to avoid worry completely, there are actions that can be taken—either as an overall life strategy or through advanced planning for particular circumstances—that can be useful in controlling worry. This chapter will help you use worry as a signal for when you need to make a change and will provide strategies for planning in advance and developing a lifestyle for yourself that reduces worry to a minimum.

Advance Planning Strategies

Let's face it—a lot of people do some really bizarre advance planning that seems, in some strange way, to be comforting. I will never forget the woman who told me that one snowy night her husband, a truck driver, was late coming home for dinner. As she waited for him, she convinced herself that his truck had gone off the road into a ravine and that he had been killed. By the time he walked in the door, an hour or so late, she was already planning the hymns they would sing at his funeral. Did this help? It certainly filled her time while she was waiting. And she was preparing herself for the shock she "knew" was coming. In this case she might have better used her time engaged in some distracting activity like reading an absorbing book or working on a creative art project. Her response is not the kind that will be encouraged in this advance planning section—but it's good to keep a sense of humor about these things.

Constructive advance planning will help you alleviate your worries, not exacerbate them. You can use your understanding of your worry pattern to plan for situations you suspect will cause you worry. You can use this technique for anything from dealing with the stressful drive to work to coping with an illness in your family. For example, if you know that every Friday you have an early morning meeting at work, and every Friday your drive to work is riddled with worry about being late, you can do some advance planning to ensure not only that you won't be late, but that you won't be worried about being late during your entire drive to work. You might go to sleep an hour earlier on Thursdays, so that you can wake up and leave your house an hour earlier on Fridays. If you know that you're not very good at waking up early, you might ask a friend to call you in the morning to make sure that you've gotten out of bed. Whatever you choose to do is up to you and is specific to your needs; but following this simple principle of planning in advance will save you a lot of wasted worry time. When terrible events and circumstances come up in your life, they bring along with them what feels like uncontrollable worry. Extensive advance planning can help in these dire circumstances.

When Nancy learned that her husband had a terminal illness, she made a conscious effort not to let her grief take over. The doctor told her that her husband would live several more years, but that during that time his health would gradually decline. After she got over the shock of this dire prognosis, she decided that it was important to take some action while her husband was still doing fairly well. She knew there would be certain things that might become necessary to do but that would be more difficult to address after the illness had progressed. She was aware of her own worry habit and knew that not doing these things would cause her unnecessary worry.

Nancy conferred with family members and friends to develop a plan. Some of the changes would necessitate using money that had been saved for other purposes, but she decided the actions were so important that her priorities needed to change and the money needed to be spent. The actions she took included:

- Educating herself and family members through research and attendance at support groups so they knew what to expect

- Making sure she had plenty of good support during this difficult time (she invited friends to a luncheon, described the situation and told them what she would need from them)

- Stocking up on canned and frozen foods, cleaning supplies, and paper products, to avoid emergency shopping trips

- Purchasing ample supplies of night wear, undergarments, shoes, and easy-care outfits for herself and her husband, so choosing and caring for clothing would not become stressful

- Making sure the family vehicles were in good working order with at least half a tank full of gas at all times (Who needs to worry about car repairs and running out of gas when in a crisis situation?)

- Taking care of personal health maintenance chores—annual physical, dental work, eye examination, etc.

- Making renovations to their home that would make things easy, convenient, and accessible for her husband such as wide doorways, ramps, levers on doors to make them easy to open, and grab bars in the bathroom

- Making major purchases that would increase levels of ease and comfort, like a television with a remote control and a lounge chair

- Listing easy, enjoyable day trips and other activities that could be used on good days to increase the quality of the time they had left to spend together

- Making arrangements with family members to ensure that someone was always with her husband during important medical consultations so instructions and recommendations were clear

When the going got really tough, Nancy found it helpful to repeat over and over the Serenity Prayer:

> Grant me the serenity to accept the things I cannot change, the courage to change the things I can, and the wisdom to know the difference.

By the time the situation had become very serious, Nancy was ready. It wasn't easy, but it was much easier than it might have been. There was much less worry than there would have been if she hadn't done a good job of advance planning.

Now, several years after her husband's death, Nancy says that the advance planning was a lifesaver for her throughout his illness. Having taken care of a lot of little worries, like "What do I have to wear?" and "Is there any food in the house?" she was able to focus on the important tasks involved in caring for and supporting her husband.

Some other life circumstances that might benefit from this kind of extensive advance planning include

- Preparation for a child to leave for college

- Advanced age

- A wedding, holidays, or other celebrations

- A birth

- A disabling illness

- Impending surgery

- Moving

- A job change

- Home renovations

- Having guests

- A major, time-consuming special project like a doctoral thesis

One woman in the study said,

> I plan ahead a lot to relieve or avoid worry. For example, I always try to have enough food—good food—on hand. On weekends I prepare a few meals for the week so when I get home between 5:30 and 7 in the evening, I'll have good food available and I won't eat junk. I clean up a little every day so that I don't feel overwhelmed with household chores—a little at a time is my motto.

Is there a circumstance in your life that could benefit from advance planning to control worry?

_____ Yes

_____ No

If so, describe the circumstances.

_____

_____

The following work sheet might help you control this worry. You can make as many copies of this work sheet as you think you'll need.

Advance Planning Work Sheet

Describe anticipated event or circumstance:

_____

_____

_____

When will it occur, or when is it likely to occur?

_____

What actions could you take in advance to ease the situation?

_____

_____

First Action

_____

When do you need to take this action?

_____

Who will you need to ask for help to get this done?

_____

How will you implement this action?

_____

_____

How will taking this action help relieve your worry?

_____

_____

What purchases, if any, need to be made?

_____

_____

If you don't have the money readily available to make these purchases, how could you get it (credit cards, loan from a bank or family member, savings, and so on)?

_____

_____

_____

Next Action

_____

When do you need to take this action?

_____

Who will you need to ask for help to get this done?

_____

How will you implement this action?

_____

_____

_____

How will taking this action help relieve your worry?

_____

_____

_____

What purchases, if any, need to made?

_____

_____

_____

If you don't have the money readily available to make these purchases, how could you get it (credit cards, loan from a bank or family member, savings, and so on)?

_____

_____

_____

(Make copies of this page for as many actions as you need to make.)

Reality Check

In some cases, advance planning may take the form of a reality check. If a worry is bothering you, you might want to take the time to determine whether or not the worry is likely to become a reality. Rather than spending your time and energy feeding the worry with possible negative outcomes, really consider what it is you're worrying about and whether or not you can do anything about it. If it's something unlikely and that you can't do anything about, like a meteor hitting Earth, for example, then a simple reality check will help you let go of the worry. Here are some questions to ask yourself when you're doing a reality check:

- What is the likelihood of this actually happening?

- Does it help me in any way to worry about this happening?

- Is worrying about this a good use of my time and energy?

- Are there other things I would rather be doing with my time than worrying about this?

- Will I prevent this from happening by worrying about it?

- Is this worry really any of my business?

If you decide that there is a possibility that what you're worrying about can happen, and that there is something you can do to prevent it from happening, then it's time to do some advance planning or problem solving. Use the Advance Planning Work Sheet on page 91 or review the problem-solving technique in chapter 3. If you decide that either the event is unlikely to occur or there is nothing you can do to prevent it from occurring, choose some diversionary activities from chapter 4 to focus your attention away from the worry.

One warm spring night, I was walking on our country property after dark, enjoying the quiet of the evening. Suddenly I found myself worried about being attacked by an animal. After being with this worry for a few minutes, and actually considering returning to the house, I did a reality check with myself. I asked myself, "What is the likelihood of this happening?" The likelihood that this might happen, I realized, was nil. The fox, deer, and even occasional moose that inhabit our area have never been known to attack people. I have never heard of anyone being attacked by an animal, either at night or in the daytime. I took a couple of deep breaths and continued my walk.

Developing a Lifestyle That Minimizes Worry

*When you have a general plan (as long as
it's flexible) for your busy life, a lot of the
little worries or situations take care of themselves.*

Many people in the study said that a substantial amount of their worry is caused by not paying close attention to lifestyle issues. They lament that their lack of self-discipline and motivation keeps them from taking necessary action to change certain aspects of their lifestyle, resulting in excessive worry. The exercises in this section are designed to help you identify issues in your lifestyle that are causing you worry and make plans to create positive change. This is a lot like planning in advance for a specific worrisome event, only now you'll be exploring the daily issues in your life that cause worry.

Identifying Lifestyle Issues That Are Causing Worry

Certain behaviors, characteristics, and situations that have become so commonplace you don't even think about them may actually be making your worry problems worse. In the study, we asked the participants to consider their own lifestyle issues—big and small—to see which ones may actually be contributing to their worry. We came up with a pretty long list. The following list represents the most common issues people noted as problematic; check any that may be causing you worry or fill in the blanks with lifestyle issues of your own.

_____ An abusive relationship

_____ Being in debt

_____ Getting good childcare for your children

_____ Eating too much sugar and junk food

_____ Dissatisfaction with your job

_____ Lack of exercise

_____ Smoking

_____ Alcoholism

_____ Health concerns

_____ Loss of contact with friends

_____ Overuse of credit card

_____ Lack of support from others

_____ _____

_____ _____

_____ _____

_____ _____

_____ _____

_____ _____

(Don't feel you have to use all of the blank spaces.)

Defining Changes in Your Lifestyle That Would Help to Control Worry

A simple change in your daily activities may provide the relief you need. A friend of mine told me that because she was sick of always getting frustrated with other drivers and worrying about being late, she now makes the effort to leave her house five minutes earlier when driving to an appointment or to work. She has begun to feel much calmer when she arrives at work or an appointment, because when she's in her car, she's enjoying music instead of yelling at other drivers.

Not all changes will be as simple as my friend's was. Some may require a lot of hard work at first. Some will have to be broken down into several actions. And some just might not work for you. Making lifestyle changes takes an adventurous spirit and some hard work. You must be willing to give yourself the space to mess up before you get it right. But you must also be willing to make a change.

Study participants have used the following strategies to create lifestyle change:

- Breaking a problem down into small steps and tackling it a little bit at a time

- Establishing reasonable goals—set up sensible timelines for meeting these goals

- Staying flexible—be willing to check out all the options

- Using the strategies in chapter 3, "Techniques for Dealing with Worry"

- Keeping it simple—don't try to do more than there is time for

- Following the Serenity Prayer: Grant me the serenity to accept the things I cannot change, the courage to change the things I can, and the wisdom to know the difference.

- Trying to fit only what you can realistically do into any given day

- Joining a support group and attending regularly

- Limiting credit card use

- Creating a "things-to-do list"

- Letting go of old time-consuming rituals that are not necessary and that you no longer enjoy

- Keeping your living and work space uncluttered and organized

- Using the following rule to guide you in letting go of possessions: If it doesn't have a good use, isn't beautiful, and has no sentimental value, don't keep it.

- Taking good care of yourself (see chapter 13, "Health Issues")

One study participant said,

> I make sure the basics of physical life and comfort are satisfied: Enough sleep, warmth, and food. For me, if one of the primary needs are not quite met, I tend to feel irritable and focus more on negative things. When all my basic physical needs are satisfied, the little things don't really bother me.

Choosing an Issue and Making a Change

The following example illustrates a system for creating lifestyle change:

Richard reported that he was frustrated because his house was cluttered, uncomfortable, and hard to clean (so he avoided it). When we examined the issue further, we discovered that Richard had a problem with saving things and then with keeping these things organized. His yard was littered with broken, rusty appliances and equipment. He had been visited by the health department as a result of complaints from neighbors and he was worried that might happen again. Besides his longing for pleasant, enjoyable surroundings, Richard worried that friends avoided him because his home was such a mess, and in the case of a fire, the house would burn very quickly.

What could Richard do to reduce his worries? It wasn't easy to admit, but Richard knew his lifestyle had become an overwhelming burden. Using several of the suggestions in this chapter (breaking the problem down into small steps; establishing reasonable goals; setting up sensible timelines for meeting these goals; and not keeping an item if it doesn't have a good use, isn't beautiful, and has no sentimental value) Richard devised the following plan that he felt was a reasonable way to get things under control:

Plan to Achieve a Lifestyle Change

Overall goal: *Make my home comfortable, uncluttered, and organized.*

First action to meet goal: *Set up a small area for entertaining guests in the house that I will always keep neat, clean, and attractive.*

To do this, I must: *Spend an entire afternoon cleaning the living room.*

When: *By the end of next month.*

Next action to meet goal: *Begin throwing things away.*

To do this I must:

1. *Get my pickup truck fixed this week so I can use it to make trips to the dump.*

2. *Take a load of unusable things to the dump each Saturday until it is all gone.*

When: *Starting right away, and continuing every Saturday until all things that are no longer usable have been discarded.*

Next action to meet goal: *Give away the things I no longer want or need but that have some value.*

To do this I must:

1. *Invite each of my children to choose and take with them any items they want or need.*

2. *Donate to a thrift store items I can no longer use but that might be useful to someone else (one carload a week until task is completed).*

When: *Beginning right away until all of the usable but unneeded items have been removed from my home*

Next action to meet goal: *Organize the things I want to keep.*

To do this I must:

1. *Spend at least thirty minutes each evening sorting and rearranging the things I'm going to keep, until I feel comfortable with my space.*

When: *Beginning immediately and proceeding until I feel comfortable with my space.*

Choose one of your lifestyle issues that is causing you worry (refer back to the checklist on page 94 and 95):

Now review the study participants' list of changes that would help to control worry. What changes could you make in your lifestyle that would help to relieve worry? Make a list of those that would help you address the situation you have chosen.

_____

_____

_____

_____

_____

_____

Develop a plan like Richard's that you could use to make the desired lifestyle change. Break the overall goal into smaller steps. You may even have to break those steps down as well. Make copies of this page if you need more than one plan.

Plan for Creating Lifestyle Change

Overall goal: _____

Fist action to meet goal: _____

To do this I must: _____

_____

_____

When it will be done: _____

Next action to meet goal: _____

To do this I must: _____

_____

When it will be done: _____

Next action to meet goal: _____

To do this I must: _____

_____

_____

When it will be done: _____

Creating lifestyle change can be a big project. Be sure that you

- Allow yourself plenty of time to create this change

- Have plenty of support as you move ahead with your plan

- Take good care of yourself as you work to create this change

- Don't allow making this change to consume all of your life; set aside time to work on it and then spend the rest of your time doing all the wonderful things you enjoy

- Give yourself a big pat on the back for every positive step you take in creating lifestyle change—you may even want to reward yourself with an afternoon off or a special treat

7

Developing Your Personal Plan to Relieve Worry

Now that you have almost worked your way through the first half of the book, you may be feeling overwhelmed. You may feel that you want to take action but you can't quite figure out what to do.

I once worked with a group for eight days, sharing with them a wide variety of skills and strategies that others have found to be useful in relieving various kinds of psychiatric symptoms. Near the end of the workshop I began to hear some protests. People were saying things like, "This is all really great, but how do we organize it so we can use it in our day-to-day lives?" I didn't have a good answer, so I turned the question over to them. During the last few days of the workshop, we worked on creating a system that people felt they could use.

On coming to this middle point in the book, I feel the same need. You will not need to read every chapter in part 2 and you will not need to learn every technique you read about in part 1. What you need is your own plan to relieve worry. People have shared a plethora of excellent ideas they found useful in creating a plan. So I undertook the task of developing systems to use the techniques and skills for controlling worry in an organized way. Checking in with some of the people who took part in this study, I developed a format to assist you in developing a plan for yourself that will help you take the ideas you have learned in this book and others you have discovered for yourself and put them all together to create your personal plan to control the worry in your life.

I have found, in using a plan like this, that when I first develop it I must refer back to it often. Then, over time, as I become more familiar with the worries and responses, I need to refer back to the plan less and less. I remember many of the responses, and others have become integrated into my life.

One of the benefits of developing a plan like this for yourself is that if you find it isn't working for you, you can change it, trash it, develop a new one, or decide, "I don't really need this" and then rely on using your memory to address worries when they come up. You don't have to use the plan we have designed. You can design one of your own. Developing a plan is also a good way to summarize what you have learned and make some decisions to help you create desired changes in your life.

A computer is a great asset to developing your personal plan to control worry. It makes it easy to refer to and make changes. You can also use an inexpensive three-ring binder, some loose-leaf paper, and a set of tabs; or you can use a spiral notebook—whatever is most convenient for you.

On the first page of your worry plan, copy and complete the following sentence:

I need to address my worries about: _____ ,
_____ , _____ .

Fill in as many worries as you'd like to. Just because you write them down here doesn't mean you have to work on them now. You may choose to work on controlling several worries at once, or work on one for now and come back to work on the others when you have gained control of the first one. In my view, it's easier to work on one worry at a time, but the decision is up to you. Based on your decision, copy and complete one of the following statements:

I am just going to work on my worry about _____ *for now.*

I am going to work on several worries at once. They are: _____ ,
_____ , _____ .

I am going to work on getting rid of worry itself. (If this is your choice, refer to the ideas in chapter 4, "Focusing Your Attention Away from Worry," chapter 5, "Other Considerations in Solving Your Worry Problem," and chapter 6, "Reducing the Possibility of Worry.")

Now, before you even begin developing your plan, take a few minutes to do a reality check about your worry. Ask yourself the following questions for each worry you have listed and write your answers in your worry plan binder (or wherever you have chosen to keep your plan):

1. Is the worry valid?

2. Is this worry something I should be worried about? Why or why not?

3. What benefit do I get, or will I get, from having this worry?

4. Why do I want to stop worrying about this issue?

5. What makes this worry a problem?

6. What is the worst thing that could happen if my worrying becomes reality?

7. How much time and energy am I willing to put into controlling this worry?

8. How does it feel when I worry about this issue?

9. How would I feel if I didn't have this worry? What would change?

Sometimes just analyzing the worry in detail is enough to control it at a comfortable level. Or it may remind you of a single technique or several techniques that might effectively control this worry. What do you think is the best plan of action for you?

- *I think I can control this worry without developing a plan. The preceding analysis has already helped to control it.*

- *I think I can control this worry without developing a detailed plan. I will use the following techniques to control this worry.*

_____

_____

_____

- *I am going to develop a plan to relieve this worry.*

There are two basic plans to choose from:

1. *Controlling ongoing worries,* like being on time, controlling your intake of certain kinds of foods, or keeping your living space uncluttered.

2. *Controlling an overwhelming or dreadful situation,* like getting a positive HIV test, divorce, or the death of a loved one, or a *horrific event that may happen, or is anticipated, in the future,* like the death of a spouse, losing your job and source of income, or going bankrupt. These worries could be about something that will most probably happen, like children going away to school or the death of a friend with a terminal illness. Or they may be about an event in the future that is not likely to occur.

In your worry plan, write down which kind of plan(s) you feel you need to develop and write the worry it will address.

- *Plan 1, to control ongoing worries. I will address worry about*

  _____

- *Plan 2, to control worry about an overwhelming, dreadful or horrific situation. I will address worry about* _____

  _____

As you are developing your plan(s), you will need to refer back to related sections in this book. You can also decide which chapters in part 2 you want to read. Use the table of contents as your guide to activities and strategies that you may want to use in your plan(s).

I will include a sample of each kind of plan followed by a form you can use to develop your own plan. You can make copies of these forms for your use. These are monthly plans. You could set them up for shorter or longer periods of time, whatever you feel will work best for you.

Sample Plan 1: Controlling an Ongoing Worry

What is my goal?

To let go of worry about having enough money. (See chapter 12, "Financial Worries".)

How much time and energy am I willing to put into controlling this worry?

I'm willing to spend up to an hour a day on activities integrated into my daily living and whatever energy it takes for at least two weeks to control this worry.

What do I need to do every day to relieve this worry?

- *Work hard to ensure that I will keep my job.*
- *Save 10 percent of my weekly income so I have a "nest egg."*
- *Stop spending money on junk-food snacks.*
- *Stop impulse buying—make shopping lists and only purchase items on the list.*
- *Focus on living more simply and frugally.*
- *Do everything I can to take good care of myself.*
- *Spend at least thirty minutes involved in a fun or creative activity.*
- *Meditate for at least fifteen minutes.*

Other steps that might be helpful:

- *Ask my supervisor for a raise.*

- *Begin a job search for a higher paying job.*

- *Work additional hours.*

- *Get more training to facilitate getting a higher paying job.*

- *Cut expenses by ride sharing.*

- *Cut back on movies and other expensive outings.*

- *Budget my money.*

- *Set up a plan to use in case I lose my job or am faced with some major expense.*

If my worry about this issue worsens, it will help to (choose several of the following activities)

- *Write in a journal about it.*

- *Do a focusing exercise to figure out what is really bothering me and what to do about it.*

- *Do a visualization, picturing myself feeling carefree and enjoying the resources I have.*

- *Schedule some time to worry about this issue.*

- *Give the worry to some real or imagined person.*

- *Talk to someone about it.*

- *Divert my attention by playing my guitar.*

How do I feel about this worry after following the plan for one week?

I feel that I am making real progress. I know that in this job I will never have enough money to easily meet my needs and the needs of my family. I know that in order to get a higher paying job I need to work on my computer skills. I have enrolled in a course at the community college.

How do I feel about this worry after following the plan for two weeks?

I am doing great! Sticking to the things in the first section have really helped. Taking time out specifically to worry has created some real change. Not only has it helped me come up with some solutions, but I'm finding that I'm sometimes feeling really bored with this worry.

How do I feel about this worry after following the plan for three weeks?

A lot better. The college course has started, and I feel I'm doing something positive to change my situation. It's a good feeling. I have to study a lot, so I don't really have time to worry. It's hard to worry when I'm learning a new skill.

How do I feel about this worry after following the plan for four weeks?

I'm finding that many of the everyday tasks have become habits. I'm exercising fairly regularly, eating out less often (cooking is less expensive than going to a restaurant), and putting money from my paycheck into my savings account every month. I think this worry will continue to come up from time to time, but now I know what to do about it when it does come up. If it gets obsessive again, I will return to this plan.

Do I still need to work on controlling this worry?

_____ Yes

__X__ No

If so, do I need to

_____ Develop a new plan?

_____ Stick with the one I'm already using?

_____ Revise the plan I'm using?

Plan 1: Controlling an Ongoing Worry

What is my goal?

_____

_____

How much time and energy am I willing to put into controlling this worry?

_____

_____

_____

What do I need to do every day to relieve this worry?

_____

_____

_____

_____

_____

_____

Other steps that might be helpful:

_____

_____

_____

_____

_____

If my worry about this issue worsens, it will help to (choose several of the following activities)

_____

_____

_____

_____

_____

How do I feel about this worry after following the plan for one week?

_____

_____

How do I feel about this worry after following the plan for two weeks?

_____

_____

How do I feel about this worry after following the plan for three weeks?

_____

_____

_____

How do I feel about this worry after following the plan for four weeks?

_____

_____

_____

Do I still need to work on controlling this worry?

_____ Yes

_____ No

If so, do I need to

_____ Develop a new plan?

_____ Stick with the one I'm already using?

_____ Revise the plan I am using?

Sample Plan 2A: Controlling Worry about an Overwhelming or Dreadful Situation

What is my goal?

To control my worry about my positive HIV test. (See chapter 13, "Health Issues," for ideas on ways to address this worry.)

How much time and energy am I willing to put into controlling this worry?

As much as it takes.

What do I need to do every day to control this worry?

Take excellent care of myself which means:

- *Eat three good meals a day.*

- *Avoid junk food, alcohol, and sugar.*

- *Exercise for at least half an hour.*

- *Take the vitamins, minerals, and herbs recommended by my naturopathic physician.*

- *Do a forty-five-minute visualization exercise.*

- *Talk to a supportive person.*

- *Spend at least an hour doing something I really enjoy.*

- *Work on improving my self-esteem by repeating over and over to myself, "I am a great person."*

Other steps that might be helpful:

- *Talk to or see any of my healthcare professionals.*

- *Get more education for myself about a suggested treatment or medication.*

- *Go to a support group.*

- *Check out a recommended medication or treatment.*

- *Have a meal with a special friend.*

- *Plan a vacation.*

- *Get a massage.*

If my worry about this issue worsens, it will help to (choose several of the following activities)

- *Talk to an AIDS counselor about it.*

- *Do a focusing exercise to create a change in feeling.*

- *Have a daily peer counseling session of at least one hour.*

- *Do two guided imagery exercises with a tape each day.*

- *Take a day off from work and go to an art museum with a friend, paint a picture, go for a long hike with a friend, or read a good book.*

How do I feel about this worry after following the plan for one week?

I guess it's working. I have spent less time worrying and more time doing good things for myself. However, it's still really hard. I wake up in the night really worried.

How do I feel about this worry after following the plan for two weeks?

Talking with Jim at the AIDS project was really reassuring. We talked about the latest research and treatments and shared statistics about how much longer people are living with AIDS. And we talked about how to stay healthy so the HIV infection doesn't develop into AIDS.

How do I feel about this worry after following the plan for three weeks?

Somewhat better! This is tough. I am so disappointed and angry with myself that I am in this situation. The guided imagery is really helping.

How do I feel about this worry after following the plan for four weeks?

I'm still a long way from controlling this worry as much as I would like. It's hard for my family when I am worried so much of the time. But this plan has helped, and I will continue to use it, adding a new idea from time to time.

Do I still need to work on controlling this worry?

   _X_ Yes

   _____ No

If so, do I need to

   _____ Develop a new plan?

   _____ Stick with the one I'm already using?

   _X_ Revise the plan I'm using?

Sample Plan 2B: Controlling Worry about an Anticipated or Possible Future Situation

(This plan is for a forty-four-year-old man who has a tendency toward high cholesterol and a strong family history of heart disease. His father has died within the past year of complications following open-heart surgery.)

What is my goal?

To control worry about the possibility that I may develop heart disease like my father did. (See chapter 13, "Health Issues.")

How much time and energy am I willing to spend on controlling this worry?

A lot. A change of lifestyle is really going to help, and that's going to take a lot of time, energy, and maybe even some money.

What do I need to do every day to control this worry?

- *Eat the low-fat diet prescribed by my doctor.*
- *Get at least forty-five minutes of aerobic exercise.*
- *Do a thirty-minute meditation exercise.*
- *Spend at least thirty minutes doing a creative activity that I enjoy.*
- *Take the vitamin, mineral, and herbal supplements recommended by my doctor.*
- *Get at least eight hours of rest or sleep.*
- *Avoid working at my job more than eight hours a day.*

Other steps that might be helpful:

- *Talk with one of my healthcare professionals.*
- *Increase my exercise.*

- *Decrease my overall food intake to reduce my weight if it is climbing up.*
- *Learn more about preventing heart disease.*
- *Do a focusing exercise.*
- *Talk about my health worries with a friend.*
- *Repeat over and over, "I am doing everything I can to stay healthy."*
- *Schedule fifteen minutes a day to worry about this—then let go of the worry.*

If my worry about this issue worsens, it will help to (choose several of the following activities)

- *Do a visualization exercise that focuses on me as a healthy person.*
- *Spend more time doing a creative activity.*
- *Get engrossed in a good book or a trashy detective story.*
- *Learn more about preventive techniques to reassure myself that I'm doing the right thing or to change my regime.*
- *Do a peer counseling exercise at least once a day until the worry subsides.*
- *Journal for at least fifteen minutes.*
- *Do a one-hour meditation exercise with a tape as a guide.*

How do I feel about this worry after following the plan for one week?

Relieved! I am taking some action rather than sitting around worrying about possibilities.

How do I feel about this worry after following the plan for two weeks?

I feel the plan is working but sometimes it's difficult. I spent some more time learning about heart disease this week and feel I'm on the right track.

How do I feel about this worry after following the plan for three weeks?

It's hard to stick to the things I know I need to do for myself every day. I will reward myself by buying another tree for my orchard if I stick to the plan every day next week.

How do I feel about this worry after following the plan for four weeks?

Another tree for the orchard. The reward system really helps me stay with this plan. I feel that I need to continue with the plan for at least another month to really get it incorporated into my lifestyle.

Do I still need to work on controlling this worry?

   _X_ Yes

   ____ No

If so, do I need to

_____ Develop a new plan?

_____ Stick with the one I'm already using?

__X_ Revise the plan I am using?

Plan 2: Controlling Worry about an Overwhelming or Dreadful Situation or an Anticipated or Possible Future Situation

What is my goal?

_____

_____

How much time and energy am I willing to put into controlling this worry?

_____

_____

_____

What do I need to do every day to control this worry?

_____

_____

_____

_____

_____

_____

Other steps that might be helpful:

_____

_____

_____

_____

_____

_____

If my worry about this issue worsens, it will help to (choose several of the following activities)

_____

_____

_____

_____

_____

How do I feel about this worry after following the plan for one week?

_____

_____

How do I feel about this worry after following the plan for two weeks?

_____

_____

How do I feel about this worry after following the plan for three weeks?

_____

_____

How do I feel about this worry after following the plan for four weeks?

_____

_____

Do I still need to work on controlling this worry?

_____ Yes

_____ No

If so, do I need to

____ **Develop a new plan?**

____ **Stick with the one I'm already using?**

____ **Revise the plan I'm using?**

Support

When you are working on any growth-oriented activity like controlling worry, it helps to have the support of one or several family members or friends. Choose people you trust and ask them to

- Listen to you talk about what you are doing

- Validate your experience

- Encourage you

- Avoid giving you advice unless you ask them for it or they ask you first if you want advice

Someone who is dealing with a similar situation in their life can be a very good supporter. You can also support them as they work on creating change in their life.

Who could you ask to support you in implementing these plans?

_____

_____

_____

_____

_____

PART 2

Addressing Specific Worries

8

Minor Concerns—Past, Present, and Future

If I'm sleepless, I can worry about postage!

This chapter addresses those annoying, minor worries that can become so bothersome.

These are worries about things that

- Are not very serious

- Are often inconsequential

- Are not life threatening

- Will not change the course of your life

- Will not have any far-reaching effects

- May be petty

- Don't matter in the grand scheme of things

You may have some control over the circumstance or you may not be able to control it at all.

Ninety-eight percent of the people in the study admitted they worry about such minor concerns, including things they have done in the past, current situations, and projections of what may happen in the future. Those that said they *didn't* were adamant about it! One of them said,

> I used to worry about every little thing. I was an obsessive worrier. Before I went outside in the morning I worried about whether the car would start. I worried about whether my sweater would be warm enough. Would it rain? Would my boss be in a bad mood? I really focused on these things. Finally I decided to give it all up. Just take life as it comes. It wasn't an easy transition but I'm doing it.

Less than 10 percent of those who worry over minor concerns consider these kinds of worry to be a major problem, but they admit they would like to get these worries under control. Consider this response from a study participant:

> I'm late for something because I've stretched my time a little too tight and then someone sidetracks me. I'm in my car on my way to, say, picking up my son and taking him to soccer. Traffic is slow, I start cursing other people's driving. My adrenaline starts pumping, I feel tense and guilty, and I anticipate the pain of my son's irritated comments.

Following are some examples of the kinds of worries that study participants felt fit into this category:

Past (many of these fall into the category of *I should or shouldn't have* or *I wish I had or hadn't*)

- What did they think of me?

- Oh, I shouldn't have said that!

- I should've worn a different outfit.

- I should've gone to that meeting.

- I should've run for the school board.

- I should've gone out with him.

- I should've closed the door more quietly.

- I should've been nicer to my brother.

- I should've spent more time with my friend.

Can you think of any minor worries about things that happened or didn't happen in the past?

_____

_____

_____

_____

_____

_____

Present

- Will I get to the store before it closes?
- When will I get the first scratch on my new car?
- Will I have enough food for guests?
- Will the meal I just cooked taste good?
- Does my hair look right?
- Will I be late?
- Will I spill my coffee in the car?
- Will I have to wait in line at a store?
- Will I have trouble finding parking?
- Will I get everything done?
- Am I getting enough sleep?
- How can I keep up with day-to-day activities, like shopping, cleaning, and so on?
- Have I taken too long?
- Will they pay?
- Am I getting out of shape?

Can you think of any minor worries about things that are happening currently?

_____

_____

_____

_____

_____

_____

Future

- Will there be bad weather?

- Will there be enough time?

- Will my hair turn gray?

- Will I go bald?

- Will I be sick in old age?

- Will I get "crotchety" when I get old?

- Will my child finish high school (she's now four years old)?

Can you think of any minor worries about things that you project may happen in the future?

_____

_____

_____

_____

_____

_____

How to Deal with Minor Concerns

People agree that their lives would be much more pleasant if they could "let go" of all this day-to-day worry. A woman in the study described a scenario from her college days that is still vivid to her many years later.

> One day I was worried. I can't even remember what it was about—something that was going on. I "cut" a class, something I never did, because I was so worried. I was standing around in front of the library wondering if I should "cut" the next class when a friend

stopped and asked me what was wrong. I told her about this big worry. She said, "Well, just give it to me." I quickly symbolically handed it over to her, like I was giving her a huge burden, and then scurried off to class.

Other people in the study confirmed that giving the worry away, either to a real person who knows you are giving the worry to them or to a made-up person, worked very well for them.

Another woman also reported an interesting technique for dealing with everyday worries: she schedules it.

When I notice that I'm preoccupied with too much worry about what's happening in my life, I pull out my daily appointment book and set aside a "worry time." How long I give myself depends on how busy I am that day, but usually ten or fifteen minutes works very well. Then I write it in my book. For instance, from 2:30 to 2:45 I am going to worry. It effectively stops my current worry. When the time arrives, I set myself down and stew, fret, and fuss. By the time I get done (fifteen minutes can seem like a long time under these circumstances), I'm usually totally bored with the whole thing. Then I return to what I'm doing, refusing to allow myself to worry (which is much easier now that I've spent some time totally dedicated to doing it). If I'm still worrying, I may give myself another "worry time" later that day or the next day.

I find that a reality check is crucial for me in dealing with everyday concerns. For instance, I find myself worrying that I won't get to work on time even though I work for myself. There's no one checking on what time I get in. I just feel that everyone else in the world is going to start work at 9 A.M. so I should too. On the way, hurrying to work, perhaps exceeding the speed limit a bit and feeling the tension in my body, I remember to say to myself, "Wait a minute. No one is checking the time clock. You don't even have one. And if you do get in to work a few minutes late, it will have minimal impact on what you get done today. So slow down and try to enjoy the scenery."

I had some worries around the last holiday season that also responded to my reality-check method. When the holidays are approaching I usually begin to worry about when, in the midst of the holiday season, I will get time to bake the cookies. Ever since I can remember I have always baked at least five batches, and often many more, of holiday cookies. This year, the days were rapidly approaching, and I was contemplating the prospect of compromising my health and sanity by staying up late at night to get the cookies baked. Suddenly the reality-check method kicked in; it is finally becoming a habit. Several thoughts occurred to me: (1) I can't eat any of these cookies myself because I'm allergic to wheat and they all contain flour,

(2) My spouse is always fighting high cholesterol, so they are not the best thing for him, but if they are around he will surely eat them, (3) None of the kids really need them; they will get enough sugar from other sources, (4) I don't enjoy making the cookies anymore. I'm tired of it. I'd rather sit in my comfy chair and listen to Christmas music, which would be far better for my disposition, and (5) I could give all the people who I usually give a tin of my cookies a bar of nice smelling soap or a jar of maple syrup. So I didn't make any cookies! Nobody even asked for them (and here I thought it was a holiday tradition).

Here are some other methods people in the study used for dealing with everyday worries:

> I'm trying to learn "radical acceptance" of my circumstances. Rather than let everday worries overtake me, I look at them as normal occurrences that happen in life, view them as inevitable, and let go of them.

> I ask myself what I can do to create change. If I'm doing something about it, I don't worry.

> If you can manage to be very present, keeping your full attention focused on what is happening and where you are at that time, then all worries evaporate. However, this method probably won't work for worries about the present.

> If I know that it's not a big deal, I deny that there's a problem and just proceed based on that premise. It works like a charm for me.

> When I find myself obsessively worrying about day-to-day issues that don't really matter, I try to inject humor into the situation and have a good laugh at myself.

Identify a minor worry that has bothered you that you dealt with successfully.

How did you deal with this worry?

Do you think you could use this strategy again to deal with a minor worry?

_____ Yes

_____ No

Why, or why not?

_____

_____

_____

Which of the techniques in the following lists, do you think might help you let go of minor, everyday concerns?

The following techniques are described in chapter 3, "Techniques for Dealing with Worry":

_____ Focusing

_____ Guided Imagery

_____ Talking about the worry

_____ Peer counseling

_____ Journaling

_____ Brainstorming

_____ Taking action to address the concern

_____ Problem solving

_____ Changing negative thoughts, attitudes, and beliefs to positive ones

The following techniques are described in chapter 4, "Focusing Your Attention Away From Worry":

_____ Focus on detail

_____ Being present in the moment

_____ Progressive muscle relaxation

_____ Prayer

_____ Breathing techniques

_____ Diversionary activities

_____ Exercise

_____ Affirmations

_____ Helping others

Some of the ideas in chapter 5, "Other Considerations in Solving Your Worry Problem," might also provide you with some relief:

_____ Examining your physical and emotional health

_____ Eating well

_____ Getting more exercise

_____ Getting enough light through your eyes

_____ Taking vitamins, minerals, herbs, or other food supplements

_____ Homeopathy

_____ Aromatherapy

_____ Using your senses

The following techniques are described in chapter 6, "Reducing the Possibility of Worry":

_____ Advance planning

_____ Reality check

_____ Developing a lifestyle that minimizes worry

With regular practice of the methods that work best for you, you will notice that your day-to-day worries about current life circumstances will diminish.

Quick, on-the-spot responses are sometimes the best way for dealing with these kinds of worries. When you realize you are worrying about something minor, try using one of the following techniques to "nip it in the bud":

- Say one of the following statements over and over to yourself:

  "Lighten up."

  "Think about something else."

  "This is not worth worrying about."

  "This is not worth getting all steamed up about."

  "Relax!"

  "I can't change it so I won't think about it."

  "I am great."

  "I am a (wonderful, smart, pretty, witty, competent, capable, responsible, likable, etc.) human being."

- Be present in the moment. (See chapter 4, "Focusing Your Attention Away from Worry.")

- Do a deep breathing exercise. (See chapter 4, "Focusing Your Attention Away from Worry.")

- Do a reality check. (See chapter 6, "Reducing the Possibility of Worry.")

- Think about something you are looking forward to, for example, eating dinner, going to bed, watching a video, petting your dog.

- Play with your pet.

- Play with your child.

- Call and chat with a friend.

- Spend a few minutes focusing on an object, for example, a plant, picture, piece of furniture, a person's face, a piece of fruit, a pretty flower. (See chapter 4, "Focusing Your Attention Away from Worry.")

- Ask yourself the following questions:

  "Is this really worth worrying about?"

  "What is the benefit of worrying about this?"

  "Isn't there something else I could be doing with my time that would be enjoyable?"

Which of these ideas do you think might work well for you?

_____

_____

_____

_____

_____

_____

When are you going to try them?

_____

_____

_____

9

Things You Can Control and Things You Can't Control

I think that is why I have this attack mode with my worry pattern. If I perceive that hard work can fix it, I will muscle it to the ground.

Things You Can Control

People in the study said they worry moderately about things in their life that they feel are within their control. One person said, "For me the problem is knowing just what these things are—lots of trial and error trying to figure out what I can control and what I can't."

For many years I had not been clear with myself about the things in my life I can control and those I cannot control. My life was hectic, chaotic, and overwhelming. Each day I felt that I had more things to do than any one person, even a highly motivated and very energetic person, could expect to accomplish. I thought the situation was out of my control. I spent a lot of time throughout each day worrying that I wouldn't get done what I thought had to be done. I was always tense and frustrated, which made me irritable.

I was also losing sleep because I was worrying over how I would get everything done. Through counseling and deep reflection I came to understand that this lifestyle was *not* out of my control. I had the power to create a lifestyle that was not hectic, chaotic, and overwhelming. In order to do that I had to address the fact that I was being guided by the following erroneous belief patterns that I had adopted at some time in my life:

- If someone asks you to do a favor, you do it.

- It's not okay to ask for help.

- You need to be working all the time to be worthwhile.

- You need to take care of everyone else or they won't like you.

- You need to do everything perfectly.

I eliminated a lot of that worry when I realized

- I could say no when someone asked me for a favor.

- I could ask other people to help me. I could delegate (that was the beginning of a chore chart at our house).

- I could take time off to relax and still be a valuable person (what a relief that was).

- I don't need to take care of everyone else. They can learn to take care of themselves. In fact, that is a preferable situation. Amazing as it may seem, people still seem to like me.

- There are lots of things that don't need to be done perfectly.

Can you relate to the following worries that people in the study cited as things they can control?

- Lifestyle

- Living space

- Getting my life more organized

- Home repairs

- Long-term health (to some extent)

- Food and drink choices

- Smoking

- Exercise habits

- Getting enough rest

- Money spending patterns

- Driving habits

- Being late

- Relationships (to some degree)

- How I raise my child

- Having good friends

- My behavior in relation to people I care about or work with

- People I let down

- My job (Should I change it? How? When?)

- Workload and time management

- The amount of work I get done

- My achievement level

- My daily accomplishments

Here's what one study participant had to say about these controllable issues:

> To some extent, I can control my financial well-being, general health through diet and exercise, relationships through being supportive and considerate, but I worry about whether or not I will really do these things.

Do you worry about some things you could control?

_____ Yes

_____ No

If so, what are they?

_____

_____

_____

_____

Lack of motivation, time, energy, and resources, along with procrastination, not figuring out what you need to do, and sometimes plain neglect get in the way of relieving worries that could be controlled. What prevents you from controlling the things you worry about that you *could* control?

_____

_____

_____

_____

_____

Are there any erroneous thought patterns that hamper your efforts to bring these issues under control?

_____ Yes

_____ No

If so, list them here along with a positive statement you could use and act on instead of the negative one.

Erroneous Thought Pattern   **Positive Response Statement**

_____   _____

_____   _____

_____   _____

_____   _____

_____   _____

_____   _____

     As is usually the case for most people, when I tried to change my erroneous thought patterns to positive ones, I often found myself reverting back to the familiar erroneous thought patterns. It takes persistence and ongoing repetition of positive responses to change these thought patterns. There are many excellent exercises that can help you change these negative thought patterns to positive ones. (See chapter 3, "Techniques for Dealing with Worry.") Other activities listed in chapter 3 can also help in relieving worries about issues you can control.

     You could also choose to develop a plan, like the one that follows, to create change in your life that would address and control specific worries. The example is followed by a form that you can use to develop your own plan. Or better yet, you can develop a form of your own.

Sample Plan to Deal with Worries about Things You Can Control

Issue:

     Lack of exercise. I'm worried that my muscles are getting flabby and that I'm increasing my chances of getting osteoporosis because I don't exercise enough.

(Someone told me that losing a day's exercise is equivalent to smoking a pack of cigarettes every day; I don't know if that's true, but I decided that believing it would keep me on track.)

Goal:

Twenty-minute walk or some other type of exercise three days a week, one-hour walk or some other vigorous exercise twice weekly, stretching five minutes daily.

Steps to take in week 1:

- *Two twenty-minute walks*

- *One long walk (at least forty-five minutes)*

- *Three five-minute stretching times*

How will it feel if I take these steps?

Really great!

What's keeping me from taking these steps?

Feeling like I don't have enough time and not making it high enough of a priority.

What can I do to eliminate those factors?

At least twenty times daily, repeat the affirmation, "I have time to exercise. It is very important."

When and how will I put my plan into action?

I'm going to do it starting today. I will repeat the affirmation every morning. Then I will take the twenty-minute walks on Tuesday and Thursday, the long walk Sunday afternoon with my friend Iva, and I will stretch Monday, Wednesday, and Friday morning before my shower.

Have I achieved what I set out to accomplish the first week?

Yes!

Based on that information, I am going to make the following plan for week 2:

- *Twenty-minute walks Monday, Wednesday, and Friday*

- *A long walk Thursday afternoon and Sunday afternoon*

- *Stretch every morning*

How will I feel if I take these steps?

Stupendous!

What's keeping me from taking these steps?

Not setting aside time!

What can I do to eliminate those factors?

Make appointments in my date book to exercise and keep them.

Have I achieved what I set out to accomplish the second week?

Not quite; I missed one stretch and one twenty-minute walk.

Based on that information, I am going to make the following plan for next week:

Stick to the same amount of exercise but buy myself the new sweater I've been wanting if I do it.

Continue to make further sheets for succeeding weeks until you have achieved your goal.

A Plan to Deal with Worries about Things You Can Control

Issue:

_____

_____

Goal:

_____

_____

Steps to take in week 1:

_____

_____

_____

_____

How will I feel if I take these steps?

_____

What's keeping me from taking these steps?

_____

_____

What can I do to eliminate those factors?

_____

_____

When and how will I put my plan into action?

_____

_____

Have I achieved what I set out to accomplish the first week?

_____

Based on that information, I am going to make the following plan for week 2:

_____

_____

_____

_____

How will I feel if I take these steps?

_____

What's keeping me from taking these steps?

_____

_____

What can I do to eliminate those factors?

_____

_____

Have I achieved what I set out to accomplish the second week?

_____

Based on that information, I am going to make the following plan for next week.

_____

_____

Continue to make further sheets for succeeding weeks until you have achieved your goal.

While writing this section I couldn't help but think about a situation in my life that I thought of as "out of my control" but that was really in my control: I used to have a hard time keeping my work organized. My desk was always so littered I couldn't work on it. I was always afraid I'd miss some important note or letter.

The first step I took was to purchase a computer program to keep track of names and addresses, who needs to be called when, and all the interactions I've had with that person or business. The program even has reminders that pop up on the screen when there is something I need to take care of. That was a big step forward. But things were still too cluttered on my desk, which contributed to my worry. What could I do? I came up with the following strategy:

1. I have a wonderful person on my staff who is a great organizer. I could work with her for a day or two and get all of my files and systems reorganized so I have a clear place where "everything belongs." I could store or get rid of stuff I no longer need.

2. Develop the habit of spending the first few minutes of each day, probably fifteen minutes, dealing with, putting away, or scheduling tasks related to e-mail, mail, or phone messages.

3. Develop the habit, through consistent practice, of putting things away as soon as I'm done using them.

4. Reserve a few minutes before I finish work for the day to straighten things up and put things in order.

I planned to implement this strategy at the end of the month and made the following list for myself:

1. Set up the reorganization time with my staff person and schedule two days to do this work.

2. I respond well to a "gold star system," so for each day that I successfully complete steps 2, 3, and 4, I will give myself a gold star. I will stick it on the calendar. When I have done it successfully for two weeks I will take my spouse out for dinner at our favorite restaurant.

3. To be sure these habits will really stick, I will have the same reward at the one-month mark.

I got off to a rocky beginning when I kept rescheduling the reorganization time, but once I got past that part, the plan worked well. It was hard not to get back into my old habits when I was pressed for time, but eventually the new behaviors became habits.

Good luck on relieving your worries about things that you can control.

Things You Can't Control

*I have worries regarding the happiness and health
of my children. But, since they are grown, I have
little influence over whether they eat and sleep well,
what they do, their relationships, and their children.*

Worries about things we can't control are very frustrating. Sometimes these conditions exist for years, even for a lifetime. One of the people in the study said, "These worries tend to spin off into anxiety attacks because I can find nothing to do to address them. So they feel very big." Another said, "It has been a struggle to admit what I can't do and let go of it."

In the study, the outstanding issue that many people cited as one they couldn't control, and one that they worried incessantly about, was offspring. They worry about the health, well-being, and happiness of their children, who they continue to worry about, even as the children reach adulthood. As their children have offspring of their own, many of them broaden their circle of worry to include their grandchildren. And, as anyone who has children knows, this worry is absolutely useless. You cannot affect your children's or grandchildren's lives with your worry. Some of the specific and "heavy" worries around this issue that were shared by study participants included the following:

- Accidents

- Addiction problems

- Sexual preference issues

- Education and career choices

- Location and housing choices

- Job availability

- Making the best use of their abilities

- Relationships

- Rejections, disappointments, and bad luck

- Illnesses

Estrangement from children, cited in some cases, served to increase the intensity of the worry.

Add to this list worries about other things we can't control, such as

- Certain difficult family issues—divorce, illness, and so on

- War

- Prejudice

- Capital punishment

- Violence, crime, and juvenile delinquency

- Economic issues

- Accidents

- The behavior of others

- Certain health problems

Do you have worries about things you can't control?

_____ Yes

_____ No

If so, describe them.

_____

_____

_____

_____

_____

Such worries are a heavy burden for people. How do you live your life in a peaceful, calm way when you are so often overwhelmed with worries about things that are totally out of your control? People report that worries about things they can't control have contributed to illness and the ending of close relationships, and has inhibited their ability to work or meet their goals. How do people deal with these worries, which, when they become obsessive, can seriously affect the quality of their lives?

One study participant suggested involving yourself in something that requires mental, physical, and spiritual activity and where you participate in the creation of something positive—like music, visual art, or a written work.

Here are some other ideas:

- Do the best you can to develop an enjoyable, rich, and rewarding life and lifestyle. (See chapter 5, "Other Considerations in Solving Your Worry Problem.")

- Find some kind of meditation, relaxation, or stress reduction routine that works for you. (See chapter 3, "Techniques for Dealing with Worry.")

- Spend time involved in a pleasurable activity.

- Initiate an intensive study of a topic that interests you.

- Set aside time every day to spend with people you enjoy.

- Become involved in a volunteer activity.

If worry about things you can't control is an issue for you, do you think any of the preceding ideas would help you deal with these worries so they don't interfere with the quality of your life?

_____ Yes

_____ No

If so, which ones?

_____

_____

_____

_____

_____

Can you think of other ways you could keep these worries from affecting the quality of your life?

_____ Yes

_____ No

If so, what are they?

_____

_____

_____

_____

_____

One woman in the study who feels she no longer has to worry about things she can't control says,

> Now I'm really at an excellent phase. Children grown and doing well, enough money, a rewarding job, a solid marriage, and just recently a chestnut horse!

Such a lovely phase to look forward to! Remind yourself that your life can be more like this, and then take steps toward your own dreams.

10

Serious Life Situations and Possible Future Circumstances

When I found out my son had a rare blood disorder, I was absolutely consumed with worry. It immobilized me. I needed to take action and make some decisions and I couldn't do it.

Often, people think of worry and the issues that cause worry as more of a nuisance than anything worthy of much attention. However, sometimes there are circumstances so serious and desperate that they totally consume you. The outcome of such situations can change your life forever. You may experience loneliness, grief, and deep despair. One-third of the people in the study admitted that much of their worry is related to these kinds of situations.

While you may or may not be able to do anything about the situation, the way you deal with the worry about such a situation can make a difference in your ability to make good decisions and stay both physically and emotionally well while the situation is most intense. Since these situations can go on for long periods of time, often years, it is even more important to address the situation in a way that is in the best interests of all concerned.

Serious Life Circumstances

Beth's situation with her husband, John, had become intolerable. John's constant alcoholic rages, along with physical and emotional abuse, convinced Beth that she had to leave with her two children, ages twelve and four. She moved out of the city they had lived in and talked John into agreeing to a divorce. When she returned to the area so her children could visit with their father, John, already remarried, filed suit to gain custody of the children. Through a long and hostile trial, John lied and connived until he convinced the judge that Beth was an unfit parent and that the children should stay with him, allowing her only very minimal opportunities to be with her children.

Beth was concerned for the well-being of her children. She feared that they too would be the victims of John's abusive behavior. So she made a decision that she would flee and hide out with the children. She left with her daughter (her son was unwilling to leave) and began a desperate journey that spanned many years, living on the run and hiding out in remote areas.

Beth's most significant worry during that time was being found and having her daughter turned over to her husband. Additional worries included the possibility of being jailed for kidnapping, and trying to raise a young daughter in such unsettled circumstances.

I asked Beth how she dealt with the extreme worry that she experienced. She said that she really let her creative abilities carry her through the difficult time. She journaled extensively. She focused on her drawings. The drawings that she shared with me depict her agonies through that time. Her guitar became her good friend, giving her countless hours of relief as she played and sang popular songs and songs that she had composed.

Rob, a young man in the study, also found himself in a desperate situation.

> When I was twenty-two and information about AIDS was just becoming available, my lifestyle and unexplained health problems convinced me that I was HIV positive. I became consumed with worry and fear. These were worries and fears based in a reasonable reality. I was worried that I would lose my health insurance and that I would be unable to get treatment. I also worried about dying before getting to experience life, the pain and ugliness of this horrific disease, and who would take care of me when I could no longer care for myself. I had been planning to go to school and begin a career. I no longer knew what to do, how to plan for a future I was afraid I wasn't going to have.

I had to come up with some coping strategies that I felt were going to be necessary to get me through "the rest of my life." I didn't want to spend whatever time I had left consumed with worry. The first thing I did was to learn T'ai Chi. Actually I got roped into it by a friend, but it didn't take long for me to realize how important it was to my peace of mind. The goal of T'ai Chi is to have no fear and to be present in the moment. I had to be aware of my body and mind and how to connect them. T'ai Chi was virtually a lifesaver for me.

In addition, I had good friends around me who were going through the same thing. There was a lot of mutual support in the gay community. This offset the rejection experienced by so many people. I had additional support from my three sisters. I lost the fear that no one would ever want to be with me.

I read every self-help book that came out. I felt that I bonded with a lot of the teachings, particularly those that showed me what tied me down in my own fears and how I allow society to tell me what to do rather than doing what I want to do. I also decided that to get the most out of whatever life I had left, I needed to eat well and take better care of myself.

I lived for three years assuming that I had AIDS. When anonymous AIDS testing came out, I finally went and had a test. I couldn't believe it when the results came back negative.

Following are some serious life situations. Have you ever experienced, or are you now going through, any of the following circumstances?

_____ Loss of a close family member

_____ Ending a close relationship or having a relationship ended by the other person

_____ Having a family member or close friend with a serious or terminal illness like Alzheimer's disease or AIDS

_____ Experiencing symptoms that indicate you have a serious or terminal condition

_____ Having a serious or terminal condition or illness like a brain tumor, colon cancer, breast cancer, multiple sclerosis, and so on

_____ Having a disability

_____ Having a family member or close friend who was critically injured in an accident

_____ Losing all of your financial assets

_____ Losing your home or other possessions through foreclosure

_____ Losing your home and possessions through a fire or other disaster

_____ Having serious trouble with the law

_____ Being unfairly accused of a crime

_____ Being the victim of a crime

_____ Being responsible for someone else getting hurt or killed

_____ Being very poor

_____ Knowing, or suspecting, that people you love are in an abusive relationship

_____ Being deeply depressed or experiencing severe psychiatric symptoms

_____ Spending time in an area where there is a lot of criminal activity

_____ Experiencing your own substance abuse or that of a close friend or family member

Addressing and relieving these kinds of worries is much more difficult and needs more drastic action than when addressing worries about minor concerns. In many of these circumstances you may need to have all of your capacities at peak level to allow you to make good decisions and take appropriate action. Often your mind may be so clouded with worry, it's difficult to concentrate and think clearly. Or you may stretch yourself to the limit in order to be there for someone else, only to "fall apart" later. Relieving worry is not only helpful in serious situations, it may be absolutely essential to allow you to do the things you need to do.

Maria has three adult children (all in their twenties). Her youngest daughter, Alyssa, married a man who, although he seemed pleasant and rather charismatic at first, began verbally abusing her about three months after the marriage. He ranted and raved about her "faults," constantly assaulting her confidence and her belief in herself as a worthwhile person. He tried to control her every move and even to limit her time with her close friends, or to keep her from seeing them at all. At first, Alyssa thought he might be right, and that if she could only "try harder" he wouldn't be so abusive. Between episodes of verbal abuse, he treated her in a very loving way. The situation was confusing and distressing to Alyssa, and frightening to family members as they became aware of the severity and danger of the situation. Before long he started threatening, pushing, and hitting her.

Maria knew her daughter's life, the lives of her grandchildren, and even the lives of other family members were in danger. She, of course, became very worried. She had a hard time focusing at work. Tasks that were usually easy for her seemed much more difficult. Decision making and problem solving felt impossible. What could she do?

Maria used the following framework to help deal with her difficult situation. Look it over and see if it would be helpful for you. If you think it would be, you can use the blank form that begins on page 148. The order in which you do these things, and those you choose to do, depends on your situation.

1. Ask yourself the following questions:

   - "Is there anything I can do to improve or correct the situation?"

   - "Am I willing to do it?"

   - "Is it in my best interest, or the interests of others who are involved, to do it?"

   - "Do other people involved want me to do it?"

2. To help you answer the preceding questions and increase your understanding of the situation, you may have to gather information. You can use the following suggestions:

   - Call a help line (also known as a hot line) for information, resources, support, and referrals to related services. (If you can't find a general help line number or one that deals with your situation, you can find out if there is an 800 number you could call by calling [800] 555-1212.)

   - Contact community agencies that specialize in dealing with similar situations.

   - Check out the other resource books listed in this book.

   - Look up a topic related to your situation on the internet.

   - Talk to a counselor or specialist in a related field.

3. Take good care of yourself so you feel well enough to cope with this higher level of stress.

4. Keep as much structure in your life as possible so you don't have the added worry of feeling as though your life is out of control. Here are some suggestions:

   - Try to get up and go to bed at the same time every day.

   - Eat meals on a regular schedule.

   - Stick with other routines, such as an exercise schedule.

5. Get plenty of support for yourself. Keep in close touch with family members and friends who are affirming and validating. Let them

know what you need (and don't need) from them. Avoid people who are hard to deal with. You may want to attend a support group; these are usually listed in daily and weekly newspapers.

6. Don't forget to do the things you enjoy. Neglecting these things can't help and will only make you feel worse. Go ahead and do whatever it is that makes you feel really good. Paint a picture, write a poem, knit a scarf, build a birdhouse, plant another row of peas, strum on your guitar.

7. If the situation looks like it may go on for a long time, and worsen over time, as in the case of an elderly relative with Alzheimer's disease or a friend with AIDS, you may benefit from some advance planning (see chapter 6, "Reducing the Possibility of Worry"). Before the situation becomes more serious, you may want to get in extra supplies of food and certain items of clothing, get the car repaired, take care of that cavity you've been neglecting, purchase the recliner your mother has always wanted, or take your friend on that long postponed trip to the mountains.

Maria decided that in order to answer the questions in step 1, she needed to get more information. She gathered information by calling the local battered women's help line. They provided her with specific information about abusive situations and directed her to the local women's crisis center. She visited with a counselor there and discovered additional helpful resources. Maria supplemented this information with data she downloaded off the internet.

Using this information, Maria asked herself the questions in step 1 and came to the conclusion that she would talk to her daughter. She felt that she now knew how to do it in a way that would engage Alyssa while avoiding compromising her safety. Maria had the support of her family members in taking this action. In talking with her daughter she was able to discuss places Alyssa could go and places she could call if the situation became unsafe. Maria also talked to her in a nonthreatening way about leaving the situation. Eventually Alyssa fled with her children and spent several months in the crisis center before moving out of the area.

As the situation began to resolve itself, Maria took the following steps to keep her stress and worry levels under control:

• She took good care of herself by eating well, exercising regularly, and getting ample rest.

• She did the best she could to maintain the usual structure in her life—going to work on time, eating at regular times, and getting to bed at a reasonable hour.

- She shared the situation with supportive friends and attended her women's support group.

- She planted a small garden, which she tended daily, and got out to an occasional movie or theater event.

When she was in her early thirties, Sue found a small lump in her breast as she was showering. Here's how she reacted:

> My immediate reaction was panic. Was it cancer? Would I need long, involved chemotherapy? Would I lose my hair? Would I live to see my kids grow up? Would I die? I recognized that this train of thought wasn't getting me anywhere. I called my physician and arranged for an examination. Unfortunately my physician was out of town so I couldn't get an appointment until the following week. Rather than continue to worry about the "what ifs," I decided this was a good time to divert my attention by taking a family trip to the museums in the city for the weekend, arranging several get-togethers with close friends, and beginning work on a long-envisioned rock garden.
>
> My doctor's visit confirmed my fears. A biopsy was the next best step. Another wait in which I focused my attention on my kids, fun activities, taking good care of myself, and really going "great guns" on the rock garden. In addition I checked out several good books on breast cancer and surfed the internet for further information.
>
> Over the next few weeks I underwent a biopsy, follow-up surgery, and chemotherapy. It all seems like a blur now. I was constantly trying to fend off incessant worry so I could study new information as it came in, talk things over with my friends and family, and make good decisions for myself. Now that's behind me but the worry is still here. As far as the doctors can tell I am cancer free. But they won't really give me an all clear for five years.
>
> Between my six-month checkups, I try to live my life to the fullest and keep the worry that tries to creep in at bay. I'm using lots of the breathing, relaxation, and stress reduction exercises everyday and sticking to a tight diet, and an exercise and rest routine. The rock garden is glorious. I'm exploring some new areas of interest in my life and am playing the piano again, something I haven't done for years. I've stocked the pantry and the freezer with easy-to-prepare meals to make it easy on my family in case I need another hospitalization. I've also got my affairs in order in case the worst happens.

Do you currently have a very serious situation in your life that could affect you and others you care about for a long time or the rest of your lives?

_____ Yes

_____ No

Describe the situation.

_____

_____

_____

_____

_____

Does this situation cause you to worry excessively?

_____ Yes

_____ No

If it does, does this excessive worry hamper your ability to cope?

_____ Yes

_____ No

If you answered yes to either of the preceding questions, the following form, which Maria used to deal with her situation with her daughter, may help you decide how to deal with this situation in a way that keeps the worry level as low as possible. Choose to complete the tasks in the order that works best for you.

1. Ask yourself the following questions:

"Is there anything I can do to improve or correct the situation?" (See Chapter 3, "Techniques for Dealing with Worry.")

_____ Yes

_____ No

If so, what could you do?

_____

_____

_____

"Am I willing to do it?"

_____ Yes

_____ No

"Is it in my best interest, or the interests of others who are involved, to do it?"

_____ Yes

_____ No

Why or why not?

"Do other people involved want me to do it?"

_____ Yes

_____ No

Why or why not?

2. Do you need more information?

_____ Yes

_____ No

If so, where are you going to get it?

_____ A help line

Which one? _____

Phone number _____

_____ Community agencies

Which ones? _____

_____ Resource books

_____ Look it up on the internet

_____ Talk to a counselor or specialist in a related field

Who? _____

When? _____

3. How will you take good care of yourself so you feel well enough to cope with this higher level of stress?

_____

_____

_____

_____

4. How will you keep structure in your life so you don't have the added worry of feeling as though your life is out of control?

_____

_____

_____

_____

5. How will you get support for yourself?

_____

_____

_____

_____

6. Don't forget to do the things you enjoy.

What _____   When _____

What _____   When _____

What _____   When _____

What _____   When _____

7. If the situation looks like it may go on for a long time, and worsen over time, you may benefit from some advance planning (see chapter 6, "Reducing the Possibility of Worry"). What type of advance planning will you need?

_____

_____

_____

Possible Future Circumstances

Worrying about possible future circumstances and events is a concern of many people who want to relieve their worry habit. Again, this is an area where I personally have plenty of practice. I know that there are times when I feel absolutely consumed with worry about my kids. I can envision a whole host of bizarre things that might happen to them. And, although my work is going very well, I lay awake at night worrying about whether my good fortune will continue.

People who responded to the questionnaire and attended the focus groups unanimously expressed their concern over the futility of worries about the future. All agreed that unless there is some kind of action that can be taken to prevent the anticipated scenario, this kind of worry has no value.

One woman who admitted she worries about future concerns said,

> Yup, I worry about all my current worries getting worse. I worry about my health and what would happen to my son if I died or became incapacitated. I worry about my son's passage into adulthood and if he'll have all the skills he needs.

Future circumstances that people in the study said they worry about include the following:

- Life choices and goals

- Outcomes of current difficult situations

- Aging and accompanying concerns (location, health, appearance, incapacitation, retirement)

- Emotional stability

- Illness, disability, or death of loved ones

- Health (personal, children, and other family members)

- Losing a job, future employment options

- Continued availability of financial resources

- Family members who are traveling (accidents)

- Life circumstances of family members

- Approval of others, especially family members and close friends

List other future circumstances that you worry about.

- _____

- _____

- _____

- _____

- _____

- _____

Let's look at an example of how one man dealt with worry about a possible future circumstance. The following quotation shows how Sean dealt with obsessive worry about the stability of his marriage:

> My wife, Rebecca, and I get along well and have many interests in common. Our relationship is romantic and secure. We have lots of fun together and are happily making plans for our future. We recently purchased the home of our dreams. I entered this relationship with great trepidation because my first wife left when I least expected it (I was totally devastated). This obsessive worry that my new wife will leave me continues to haunt me. Rather than appreciating what I have now, my days often are consumed with worry and fear. I lay awake at night worrying about "what ifs." Where would I go? What would I do? Would I be able to handle it? Would I be able to continue to work? Would I end up on "the street"? I want to let go of this whole thing. I want to live in the moment, appreciating what I have right now.
>
> I checked in with myself. Was there anything I could do to prevent the situation I worried about from happening? I was paying very close attention to every aspect of the relationship. Rebecca and I talk regularly to assess where we are with each other. Our lives are lovingly focused on each other. All I can really do is continue the same course.
>
> I decided that in the daytime I could relieve these worries when they come up by engaging in activities like playing my guitar, working on a writing project I enjoy, or getting involved in a project at work. A good run is often effective. I have also found some relaxation and breathing exercises to be helpful. I'm looking into taking a yoga class.
>
> I have addressed the related insomnia by taking an amino acid and a B vitamin supplement and drinking chamomile tea before going to bed. If I can't get to sleep or I awaken during the night, a progressive relaxation exercise and homeopathic chamomile help me get back to sleep.

Claudia, a mother who became preoccupied with worry about her son's ability to take care of himself when he went to college, also effectively controlled her worry about a possible future circumstance. She envisioned him getting into all kinds of trouble—using drugs, becoming an alcoholic, getting into an automobile accident, neglecting his studies and flunking out, getting his girlfriend pregnant, and so on. Her son was a top student whose conduct had always been admirable. However, she felt that away from home he would be tempted by all his friends to use bad judgment and get into serious trouble.

Through several sessions of peer counseling and sharing her worry with friends, Claudia realized that this worry was useless, had no basis in reality, was causing her some gastrointestinal distress, and was keeping her from enjoying herself. It was time to make some changes.

She examined her life and realized that it wasn't very full, that she had too much time on her hands. She decided to take a painting class. She hadn't painted in years but when she had she had thoroughly enjoyed it. Participating in the class really helped; not only did it help her take her mind off her son, but it gave her the opportunity to meet new people with an interest similar to her own. Claudia also began volunteering twice a week at the local senior citizens' center, setting up activities and helping with transportation. She even began to look into finding a part-time job in merchandising. Now whenever the worry about her son comes up, she takes note of it, reminds herself it is not based in reality, pushes it away, and keeps herself busy.

Do you have any worries about future circumstances that you would like to let go of?

_____ Yes

_____ No

If so, what are they?

_____

_____

_____

_____

Is there anything you can reasonably do to prevent the circumstance you are worrying about?

_____ Yes

_____ No

If so, what is it and when do you plan to do it?

_____

_____

_____

_____

_____

_____

If you feel sure that there's nothing you could do to prevent this possible future circumstance, and that this worry about an unknown is a waste of time and energy, I do not recommend using techniques and strategies for addressing the worry. Instead, those activities that divert your attention away from the worry are more useful. (See chapter 4, "Focusing Your Attention Away from Worry.")

Which of the following techniques, skills, or strategies (taken from chapters 4 and 5) will you try to help you let go of worries about future circumstances?

_____ Focusing on detail

_____ Being present in the moment

_____ Progressive muscle relaxation

_____ Prayer

_____ Breathing techniques

_____ Diversionary activities

List possibilities:

_____

_____

_____

_____

_____ Exercise

_____ Affirmations

_____ Helping others

_____ Vitamins, minerals, herbs, and food supplements

_____ Homeopathic remedies

_____ Other "natural" remedies

_____ Dietary changes

Other ideas: _____

_____

_____

_____

_____

_____

Letting go of these worries takes consistency and persistence. It helps to

- Write the worry down,
- Make a daily record of what you are doing to keep the worry in check.
- Evaluate your progress.

11

Global Concerns, Crime, and Safety

I used to worry a lot about global issues, but I realized that worry about nuclear disaster, global warming, and so on isn't useful because these systemic conditions are beyond our control, but not beyond our influence.

Global Concerns

Worry about global concerns affects the lives of many people. However, unless there is an intense worldwide or regional situation in progress, such as the Gulf War, most people seem less obsessed with these worries and more capable of setting them aside. Others said they try not to think about them because they feel powerless to change the situation. Several study responses indicate this clearly:

> I feel so helpless to make an impact on a global level that I tend to stay uninvolved and less worried.

> I worry very little about global concerns and have even stopped watching the nightly news because the violence was affecting me too much.

I used to worry more about these concerns, but now I'm a fatalist. We're probably going to pollute ourselves to destruction one way or the other—but how soon, I don't know.

Human beings behave atrociously. How much worse will things get, how much more abuse, neglect, devastation will we do to each other and the earth—and what positive difference can I make?

Call me selfish, I have to feel the breath of the wolf on my neck before I worry. And I'm grateful! I have so much to worry about in my personal life that I never get time to worry about global concerns!

There were a few people in the study who do worry intensively about global concerns. Often it becomes all-consuming, like those people who worked in opposition to the use of nuclear power in the 1970s and 1980s and those people who continue to work against clear-cutting in the national forests.

What kinds of global issues do people worry about?

- Over population

- Planning issues

- War

- Countries suffering the affects of war

- Hunger and famine

- Environmental degradation, pollution, global warming

- Nuclear disaster

- Social justice issues

- Disenfranchised populations

- The survival of the human race

- Oppressive governmental systems

- Future quality of life

- Terrorism

- Violence

- Human suffering and oppression

- The insensitivity of individuals toward others—homicide and mass murders, rape, the lack of personal boundaries, and lack of human dignity for self and others

Do you have worries about issues of global concern?

    ____ Yes

    ____ No

If so, what are they?

_____

_____

_____

_____

Study participants suggested the following ways of addressing worries of a global nature.

Educate yourself.
While some people felt that the less known about these topics the better, many more felt that learning all you could about an issue was preferable. That way you don't have to wonder or guess at what is really going on and you could make some decisions about any action you might want to take.

Make a financial contribution.
Many people felt absolutely overwhelmed with trying to take care of both work-related and family-related obligations along with getting some needed rest and relaxation. They felt they don't have time to do anything about an issue that they are concerned with. Their suggestion was, if you have the resources to do so, make a financial contribution to an organization that works on a concern that interests you.

Write letters, phone, or e-mail.
You can let your concerns and preferences be known to officials and other individuals who can take action in your behalf by writing letters, giving them a call, or sending an e-mail. For example, if you had a concern about air pollution from an industrial park, you could contact your city council or state environmental board. If you are concerned about how the United States is dealing with the war in Bosnia, you could contact your senators, representatives, and even the president.

Take action.
The most popular strategy for addressing these worries is to take action, and that action is usually some kind of activist work. In the early 1980s when fear of a nuclear holocaust was a major issue in the daily press, I worked to relieve my worries by joining with many others and working for the Nuclear Weapons Freeze Campaign, raising

funds to support related educational efforts. More recently, to address my worries about environmental degradation I have worked as a volunteer for a local environmental education center that monitors pollution levels in local streams.

Become a spokesperson.
Once you have learned about an issue, you can make a difference by speaking out. You can take advantage of whatever forum you find—a radio show, TV program, the newspaper, the internet—to share your views and influence the thoughts and actions of others.

Volunteer at an organization.
Organizations that work on issues of global concern are always looking for volunteers. You can be one of them. Let them know who you are and what you can do, and let them put you to work. You will feel less worried if you're doing valuable work to reduce a problem.

Run for office.
Running for office gives you a forum to speak out on issues that you care about, either locally, regionally, or nationally. If you are elected you have even more direct ways of creating change.

Ever since I was a child I worried about environmental degradation. I could see that we were using up the planet's resources at a rapid pace. My interest in these issues intensified as I got older, especially as these issues rose to prominence as national and international concerns. While I have appreciated that these issues are now getting more attention, in my view they are not getting nearly the attention or resources necessary to address them adequately.

When I was in my late thirties I began to make some life changes—some might call it a mid-life crisis. For the first time in my life I thought that, beyond raising the consciousness of my children and close associates, there was something I could do to address my environmental concerns. I enrolled in a master's program in resource management and administration in preparation for a new career in environmental protection. This new focus took me down a path of activism that has never ceased. For several years it was my full-time job. More recently I helped start an environmental education center and I volunteer whenever I can.

In addition I address global issues as time allows by advocating for people who can't advocate for themselves, using my e-mail capability to let officials know of my concerns, supporting organizations that deal with areas of concern, trying to make my votes count, and even taking part in an occasional demonstration.

Have you taken action about some issue or issues of global concern in the past?

_____ Yes

_____ No

If so, what were these issues?

_____

_____

_____

Do you think your action helped?

_____ Yes

_____ No

If so, how did it help?

_____

_____

_____

Do you feel ready to do something more to help relieve your worries about issues of global concern?

_____ Yes

_____ No

Is so, what are you going to do and why?

_____

_____

_____

_____

_____

I have learned you can make a difference in the world. I think of the words quoted by Adlai Stevenson at Eleanor Roosevelt's funeral: "She would rather light one candle than curse the darkness." If those of us who have the resources and abilities to work for positive global change do it, we can and will make a difference. What a great way to control worry worldwide!

Crime and Safety

Worry about issues related to crime and safety affect everyone. I worry every time I go up in a plane, when I am traveling on icy roads, and when I am walking in unfamiliar neighborhoods. In a world where accidents happen everyday and crime is widespread, worries about safety are to be expected. The most common safety worries mentioned in the study were about being a victim of violence or crime and being vulnerable to accidents at home or in an automobile.

Crime

> *I lived for a year or so in a very rough neighborhood in town.
> I was always wondering when the next tragedy was going to
> occur. And I worried that I might become a victim of violence
> as I walked home from the store or work. I didn't realize how
> much the sirens, noise, and general confusion were affecting
> me until we moved to the country. I feel so relieved.*

Many women in the study said that, because they are not as strong as men and because women are often the victims of crime, they worry about being the victim of violence. Their worry was echoed by gay men and lesbians who fear being the victims of hate crimes.

Being female forces me to worry about being alone in the woods or in parking garages, and so on.

Sometimes I worry about being vulnerable to the will of someone stronger than I am, especially if I perceive bad motives.

Being female affects my feelings of being threatened for my safety (rape, mugging).

I think, as a woman, I worry more about my physical safety than men do. I believe I would think a lot more about walking city streets alone at night than a man would.

Because of my sexual preference (gay man) I feel vulnerable to a hate crime.

Here are some actions people suggested to relieve worries about being the victim of violence:

- Avoid high-risk places or go there only in the company of others with whom you feel comfortable.

- Make a mental plan of what you would do to protect yourself if you were attacked.

- Keep a key between your fingers to gouge an attacker when you feel at risk.

- Carry Mace or a whistle.

- Walk in a self-confident manner, projecting self-assurance while being aware of your surroundings.

- Honor your feelings—if something feels unsafe, take precautions.

- Walk with a dog.

- Take a class or course in self-protection; learn self-defense techniques.

- Keep your car doors locked, whether you are in the car or not.

- Check in the backseat of the car before you drive off.

- Have your key in your hand ready to unlock the door when you get there.

To help keep yourself safe at home, you can do the following:

- Have a reliable system of locks for doors and windows and, if necessary, a security system; some city dwellers feel more comfortable with strong, locked iron gates or bars.

- Keep the area around your home well lighted.

- Stay in close contact with neighbors and keep their phone numbers handy.

- Work with neighbors to watch for suspicious people or activities in your neighborhood.

One woman surveyed feels uneasy when her husband is away overnight. She worries about the possibility of intruders. She and her husband have worked together to relieve her worry by installing a high-quality security system and motion sensitive lighting around the outside of their home.

Another woman said,

I used to live in a "bad" section of a large city and was afraid to go out at night. Living in a city, I learned to walk with an attitude and purpose and energetically shield myself.

A young mother said,

I never leave my son alone without knowing that the neighbors are home. Emergency phone numbers are posted by the phone.

Is there anything you could do or want to do to help relieve your worry about being the victim of violence or criminal activity?

_____

_____

_____

_____

_____

Accidents or Injury in the Home

There are many simple, commonsense precautions that may ease your worry about safety at home. Here are a few suggestions study participants had:

- Have someone around when involved in a dangerous activity like cleaning the chimney or breaking ice off the roof.
- Keep walking areas and stairs cleared.
- Close drawers when not in use.
- Keep cleaning supplies stored out of reach of children.
- Turn pot handles on the stove inward so the pot can't be knocked off the stove.
- Keep ladders, stools, chairs, and railings in good repair.
- Avoid the use of rugs that slip.
- Have smoke detectors and a carbon monoxide detector and make sure that they are in working order.
- Have electrical systems checked and upgraded.

Is there anything you could do or want to do in your home that would reduce worry about possible accidents?

_____

_____

_____

_____

_____

Automobile Safety

A man in the study said,

> Since I travel a lot, mostly on weekends, that's a bit to worry about. Especially since I travel to metropolitan areas. I try to drive consciously and carefully. In this case the worry is good, because it keeps me focused when driving. And I don't think I worry excessively about this, where it might cross the line. If it reached excessiveness, I'd look for something else to make a living.

Using common sense can help relieve worry when driving. Consider the following suggestions.

- Wear your seat belt whenever the vehicle is in motion.

- Avoid drinking when driving and don't drive when using medications that may impair your ability to drive safely.

- Avoid riding with anyone who has been drinking.

- Avoid riding with anyone you feel is not a safe driver.

- Avoid driving as much as possible when there are poor road conditions and/or when traffic is heavy.

- Maintain a speed that is appropriate to road conditions.

- Take a break from driving if you feel less than alert.

- Keep your vehicle in good repair.

- Take a safe driving or defensive driving course.

- Keep the car doors locked when driving.

- Maintain control of your personal safety if you see a dangerous situation, even if you think someone else (the driver in your or another car) is probably alert to it.

Is there anything else you could do to minimize the worry of getting in an accident when traveling?

_____

_____

_____

_____

12

Financial Worries

*Sometimes I wake up in the middle of the night filled with
anxiety. Almost always it's about money. Will we have enough
money for the mortgage, the car payment, the phone bill, the
college tuition? Do I need to find more work?*

Money is at the top of the list of specific worries. Who hasn't worried about
money at one time or other? It might be expected that people at higher
income levels would worry less about money; however, study findings indicated that the level of earnings were not an indicator of how much people
worry about money. Of the people in the study, 7 percent made under
$10,000 per year, 40 percent made $10–30,000 per year, 33 percent made
$30–50,000 per year, 5 percent made $50–80,000 per year, and 12 percent
made over $80,000 per year. Where do you fit on that continuum? _____

Do you think the level of your income affects how much you worry about
money?

_____ Yes

_____ No

If so, how does it affect you?

_____

_____

_____

While most people find this topic fraught with anxiety, a few people maintain a positive attitude toward financial concerns, making such statements as, "I don't worry about economic security" and "I refuse to worry about money." Choosing not to worry about money is one way of dealing with financial concerns. Consider these responses to inquiries about dealing with financial concerns:

> I *choose* not to worry about money—I have created my situation. If I don't like my status then I can change it. When money worries come up, I work on changing my thoughts back to positive ones.

> I believe the world is full of abundance and I have always been blessed.

> I remind myself that the universe will provide for me, and that I am already blessed with ample resources, even though they may not match what the media tell me I must have for "the good life."

> I don't think my income affects how much I worry. I've made a lot less than I do now, and I don't think I worried more then. The fact that I've had steady work over the last twenty years took worry out of my economic status.

> I find that when I worry about not having enough money, all I need to do is shift into having trust that life will provide all that I really need. Usually I'm just worrying about getting what I want rather than what I need.

Do you worry about financial concerns?

_____ Yes

_____ No

If you do, do you think you could ever just let go of that worry?

_____ Yes

_____ No

Do you think that would be a good idea?

_____ Yes

_____ No

Why or why not?

_____

_____

_____

_____

If you choose to do try to simply let go of the worry, good luck. I wish I could do it. I have tried and been unsuccessful. I find that money issues always come up for me, and my worries persist. A young man in the study echoed this sentiment:

> I'm very concerned about financial security. I'm trying to realize that there are more important things in life—health, work you love, friends, and so on. It's coming along, but it's very hard to work from that mind-set.

While most people do worry about money, the level of worries varies from minimal to extreme. The following people had some minimal worries about money.

> My concern varies, but generally this concern does not dominate my thoughts or actions. I have faith that I'll always be okay as long as I don't get greedy or live beyond my means.

> To tell the truth, I don't worry very much about my economic status. When I do feel pressed about economic matters, I usually stop spending to the extent I can and ride the thing out.

> I believe that I worry less about money because I have what strikes me as "enough" financial resources to meet my current needs and also to deal with a certain level of emergencies that may arise. However, having some financial resources is itself a source of some worries. "Am I investing my savings sensibly?" "Does this person really like me, or is she interested in my money?" (Since I don't have that much money, this latter worry almost never comes up.)

Financial concerns have a much greater effect on these people's lives:

> I am greatly affected by worries about my financial status. Many of my worries are related to something I can't afford or don't know how I'll afford. I respond by working hard. I find ways to reduce need. I complain. I work some more. I scrimp and recycle. I seek a structured plan for increasing my income. I ask for help.

> Having adequate income to meet financial commitments has been important to me. Because we do not have a budget, it has been

difficult to tailor our spending to income. I wish my spouse and I would sit down and realistically look at our income and agree upon how we would individually and together maximize our income. We can make it happen through more open discussion.

There was a time when we were heavily in debt with high interest credit cards and unable to get a mortgage (refinance). I worried about sinking in debt; we had no savings and were unable to afford medical insurance. I worried a good deal. Now that we have a better financial status I worry much less. The only true solution was to finally get a low-interest mortgage and pay off the credit cards (we keep them in the safe deposit box now). We started a savings account so we have resources in case of an emergency. I still worry a bit, not about status, but about keeping debt down.

If you're worried about financial issues and want to do something positive to reduce these worries, read on for suggestions and strategies that people in the study found to be helpful.

Financial Planning

This strategy takes time, contemplation, perhaps some research, persistence, and consistency. You'll need to follow these steps:

1. **Decide how long you want to plan for.** It might be one month, one year, or even longer depending on your age and circumstances.

2. **Set your financial goals for that time period.** For instance, if you are just starting out, your goal may be to save $1,000 over a six-month period. You may want to set some intermediate goals for shorter periods of time.

3. **Decide what you need to do to meet that goal.** It may include reducing spending, budgeting, increasing income, working more jobs/hours, or finding different work.

4. **Put your plan into action.** Whatever it is you've decided to do, you need to stick to your plan. If things don't work out exactly as you expected, you may need to backtrack a bit, but be determined to either stay the course or alter the plan as your needs change.

If you can afford it, and are serious about addressing financial concerns, you may decide to hire the services of a financial planner. People who provide this service are listed in the Yellow Pages of the phone book. Before you hire one, be sure to check their references. The best way to find a financial planner is upon the recommendation of friend.

Do you need to do some financial planning?

_____ Yes

_____ No

When are you going to begin? _____

How long do you want to plan for?

_____

What is your goal for that time period?

_____

_____

Why do you need to meet this goal?

_____

_____

What are your interim goals?

_____

_____

_____

What do you need to do to meet these goals?

_____

_____

_____

Refer to the resources section in the back of the book for additional information on financial planning.

Budgeting

The budgeting process may be part of your financial planning or it may be the only step you decide to take to resolve your financial worries. Budgeting means setting up a system for allocating the amount of money to be spent in each expense category. The budget is based on what you have spent in the past, ongoing expenses, and income. Most people, like this study participant, budget on a yearly basis.

My husband and I set up a budgeting process that has prevented a lot of grief, stress, and worry. Now we know how much money we have, and how much we can spend. Our budget helps us make good decisions about what to do next.

In order to develop a budget, you may want to purchase some budgeting work sheets at a stationery store. They usually come in a notebook form. You could also use lined paper with four vertical columns. Each line would be an income or expense category. There are two vertical columns for each month—one for the anticipated amount of income or expenses (budget) and one for the actual amounts (actual). You'll fill in the budget column for each month from your calculations and the actual column throughout the year as income comes in and money is spent. (Reserve two columns at the end for yearly totals.) Refer to the sample chart on page 174. There are computer software programs, such as Quicken, that will guide you through the budgeting process. Several of these are listed in the resources section at the back of the book.

When you're designing a budget, you'll need to follow these steps:

Step 1: Determine your anticipated income sources and list them along the left side of a budgeting work sheet.

Step 2: Fill the monthly budgeted income in the column that corresponds to the income source by estimating how much money you can expect from each of these sources in each month.

If you have one or several consistent income sources, for instance you and your partner each work in a salaried position, this can be very straightforward. It may be more difficult to project your income if you work for yourself, work on a contract basis, if you have hourly earnings that are subject to change, or have other income that is nonspecific. Most people in this position calculate their income based on a minimum estimated amount. If your income changes at different times of the year, this needs to be considered in the budgeting process. For instance, farmers and construction workers may bring in the bulk of their income during the summer.

Step 3: Figure out your expense categories and how much money you usually spend in each category in a month. Certain expenses may fluctuate, like groceries and heating fuel, or remain stable, like your mortgage or car payments. Your expense categories may include any of the following:

- Housing expenditure: mortgage or rent

- Taxes: income and/or real estate

- Heating fuel

- Electricity

- Phone
- Television cable
- Internet connection fees
- Auto payments
- Gas
- Auto repairs
- Travel
- Auto insurance
- Other insurance
- Hobbies
- Food
- Clothing
- Entertainment
- Vacation
- Savings
- IRA
- Healthcare
- Gifts

You may feel you don't need all of these categories or have others to add, depending on your circumstances.

Step 4: List these categories in a left-side column on your budgeting work sheet under the income categories.

Step 5: Fill in the amount of money you are budgeting to spend in each category in each month. You will fill in the actual amounts throughout the year as money is spent. Use amounts on past bills to calculate expense columns, using the maximum amounts. For items like heating fuel, the amount will be more in the winter months than in the summer. Make adjustments in non-essential items like entertainment and savings if your expenses exceed your income or if you go over-budget.

Step 6: Each month fill in how much you have spent on each item. You can keep a daily tally of expenses to make sure you are not exceeding budget in any area. Your checkbook and receipts can serve as an expense guide.

Following is an example of what a budget might look like:

Income:	January Budget/Actual	February Budget/Actual	March Budget/Actual
Brentwood Hospital	1500/1500	1500/1500	1500/1500
Billerica Construction	2000/1750	1000/1200	1250/1200
Thomas' Fabrics	750/750	600/600	700/750

Expenses:	January Budget/Actual	February Budget/Actual	March Budget/Actual
Mortgage	650/650	650/650	650/650
Property Taxes	200/200	200/200	200/200
Heating Fuel	75/80	60/65	50/40
Groceries	300/320	300/275	300/300

Ongoing budgeting allows you to make minor and major decisions about income and expenditures based on your past track record. This budgeting process can relieve a lot of worry and keep you on top of things financially.

Do you already budget your money?

_____ Yes

_____ No

If so, how does it help you control your worry?

_____

_____

If you don't budget now, are you going to start?

_____ Yes

_____ No

If so, how do you think it will help?

_____

_____

When are you going to set up your budget?

_____

If you have decided not to budget your money, why do you think that is a good decision?

_____

_____

Reducing Expenses

A careful review of your expenses and subsequent cutting back in some areas may be all you need to feel more comfortable about your financial situation. If you think this method might help you, keep track of all your expenses on a day-to-day basis for at least a month. Have a notebook on your bedside table and jot down every cent you spent each day. Include such things as snacks, newspapers, and cigarettes, along with essential items like groceries and fuel. After the month is up, take a look at where your money has gone. Which of these expenditures really made a difference in your life? If you spent forty-five dollars on between-meal snacks, maybe you'd prefer to save that money for a camping trip. Or maybe if you hadn't spent that sixty dollars for a new sweater you didn't really need, you could have put that money into an IRA. Your findings may be the first step in changing some habits or even in beginning a budgeting process.

Living Simply and Frugally

One choice for dealing with money problems that takes reducing expenses a little further is to live simply and frugally. You may decide that the hassle of trying to make enough money to have the lifestyle deemed so important in today's society and having to work at a job you dislike may not be worth it for you. Here's what a few study participants had to say about this:

> I treat myself well—eat good organic food, take long walks and hot baths. I try to remind myself of all the beauty I have in my life. I used to think that if I was poor my life would fall apart; I'm learning that this is not true at all.

> I decided I just wasn't willing to do it anymore. I was running myself ragged trying to keep up with a lifestyle I didn't really like. I wasn't spending enough time with my family. I hadn't painted or played my guitar in years. We bought a small place in the country, and I am working at home, making just enough money to get by. I'm happier than I have ever been.

> I have accepted the reality that my chosen work does not contribute to a high economic level and/or status.

Some of the choices you make about your life may mean ruling out things like new cars, televisions, VCRs, vacations, dining out, and wearing the newest fashions. Instead you may find yourself frequenting thrift stores or growing your own food—and being perfectly content doing that. The book *Your Money or Your Life,* by J. Dominquez and V. Robin, can help you decide if this is what you want to do. It's your life, and if you don't want to spend most of it working in a nine-to-five job that causes you worry and stress, you don't have to.

People in the study successfully reduced expenses by

- Living in an area where there is less emphasis on "keeping up with the neighbors"

- Growing and preserving vegetables and fruits

- Focusing their diet on whole foods with a maximum nutrient content rather than junk and processed foods

- Driving inexpensive used cars

- Doing their own automobile maintenance tasks like changing the oil and other fluids

- Using public transportation or walking instead of owning a vehicle

- Frequenting thrift stores for clothing and other needs.

- Not having television

- Borrowing books from libraries rather than purchasing them

- Reusing plastic containers instead of buying plastic and aluminum food wrap

- Packing lunches at home instead of purchasing them

- Taking along their own snacks when going to the movies

- Using a daycare cooperative

- Stopping smoking

- Getting rid of credit cards

- Paying off credit cards every month

- Paying off loans to avoid high interest rates

- Challenging unreasonable charges like property tax re-valuations

One study participant who is a good money manager said,

Use the money you have to generate more money. Be creative. Be aware of money and it will do more for you. Be greedy.

Do you think reducing expenses or living more simply and frugally could help you avoid worries about money?

_____ Yes

_____ No

If so, are there some changes in lifestyle you would have to make?

_____ Yes

_____ No

If there are, what are they and when do you plan to make them?

_____

_____

_____

_____

Saving

Saving money is hard for everyone. Here's what one study participant had to say about it:

> There always seems to be some immediate need or desire, some way I can rationalize not putting that money in the IRA, or neglecting the fund to pay for the degree I have wanted for so long.

If you've always thought about putting money aside but have never done it, join the club. You are not alone. However, if you are really serious about controlling your worry about money, sticking to a savings plan may need to be part of the process. Having a savings plan will ease worries because you'll always know you have money available for emergencies or for anticipated future expenses like education or retirement. Sometimes just setting aside five or ten dollars a week is enough to achieve peace of mind and a sense of security.

> I'm self-employed and work in an unstable field. So, when I have work, I'm not concerned; I get by just fine. When I'm out of work, though, I'm never sure how long it will be until I have more work. My savings really help me know I'll be fine for a while.

Do you think setting up a savings plan and sticking to it would help you control your worries about money?

If so, complete the following statement:

I am going to save $ _____ every _____ (week, month, etc.) by putting it in a _____ (savings account, money market fund, IRA, etc.) starting _____ (date). That will involve _____ (opening an account, doing some research to determine what to do, talking with a financial planner, etc.).

Changing Your Work Situation

You may decide that in order to control your financial worries, you need to make more money. How could you do that? Depending on your work it may mean

- Working more hours

- Getting another job

- Getting a different job

- Finding more work if you work for yourself

- Getting more training so you can move into a higher-paid position

- Changing careers to one that is more lucrative (more education may be needed to meet this challenge)

Do you feel you need to change your work situation?

_____ Yes

_____ No

If so, what do you need to do?

_____

_____

_____

_____

How are you going to do it?

_____

_____

_____

_____

When would you like to do it?

_____

Changing Jobs or Careers

Many people reported that they were in jobs that didn't pay enough and/or that they didn't enjoy. And yet they felt they had to continue in these jobs because they

- Didn't know if they could get other work in their field

- Felt a strong sense of commitment to their work even though they no longer liked it

- Felt they couldn't risk their own security or that of their family

- Weren't sure they could really support themselves and their family doing the things they really wanted to do

- Needed their health benefits

- Felt like they were "stuck in a rut"

- Were worried about what other people would think

- Were concerned that they might feel a loss of sense of self

Do any of these statements apply to you?

____ Yes

____ No

If so, are these concerns contributing to worry in your life?

____ Yes

____ No

What would you really like to be doing with your life?

_____

_____

_____

Is this what you are doing?

_____ Yes

_____ No

If so, great. If not, what's standing in your way?

_____

_____

_____

What could you do to change that? (For some ideas, check out the taking action, problem-solving, and brainstorming sections in chapter 3, "Techniques for Dealing with Worry," and the resources section at the back of the book.)

_____

_____

_____

I personally believe that to control worry and attain the highest level of wellness you need to **do what it is you want to do with your life**. In this process you may have to address the following questions:

Would a change in my job or career help control my financial worries?

_____

_____

_____

Is it safe for me to give up my old job before I have something else lined up?

_____

_____

_____

Should I go into business for myself?

_____

_____

_____

How long can I live on my savings?

_____

Am I ready to take this risk?

_____

_____

_____

Getting More Education and Training

Getting more education and training can be a double-edged sword. It may control your worries for the long-term, but the added expense and stress of school may increase your worries overall. Before you decide you want more education and/or training, ask yourself the following questions:

Do I really need more education and training to be able to do what I want to do in my career and my life?

_____

_____

_____

Is there a market for the skills I want to develop? (It's important to explore this issue before making an investment in education and training. You don't want to end up skilled in a field that is overcrowded or where no need exists.)

_____

_____

_____

Do I have the time, or want to take the time out of my life, to further my education? (Perhaps your life is already hectic and chaotic as it is. Maybe you don't have time to spend with people you enjoy or do the things you want to do now and expanding your education would just increase your worry about having enough time.)

_____

_____

_____

How much will it cost? Will paying for the education and training increase my worries? If I have to borrow money, will it be worth it?

Will more education and training improve my self-esteem and the quality of my life?

Am I mentally and physically stable enough to do this now?

You may not be able to answer all of these questions without some research and soul-searching. You may even want to consult with an expert. Visit your local State Office of Employment and Training for assistance. If you are looking into a college program, meet with the placement officer to find out what your prospects would be.

Study participants had varying stories about further education:

Going back to school changed everything for me. It got me out of a dead-end job and into a career that I enjoy. I love going to work. And we have enough money to live comfortably. It was rough at the time, but I have no regrets.

I decided I needed a master's degree for credibility in a field I had inadvertently stumbled into. I went back to school, trying to complete the program while working to support myself. It was a nightmare. I resented the time I spent studying. I was learning what someone else thought I should be learning, not what I really wanted to know. In retrospect, I don't feel this master's degree advanced me in any way. And I am still paying off the student loans. I really wish I hadn't bothered.

For years I thought I needed to go back to school to get more education, that I shouldn't relax until I had gotten at least a master's degree and maybe even a doctoral degree. Not getting to it was a worry that plagued me for years. Finally, I really thought about it and realized that I was happy with my life the way it was and that getting those degrees was part of living up to some old expectations from teachers and family—so long ago I can't even remember.

Do you think more education and training would help you control your worries about money.

____ Yes

____ No

If so, what is your final goal?

_____

_____

What is the next step you should take?

_____

_____

Planning Ahead

Partnerships

Several study participants who are married or in committed relationships felt that, to control their worry, they needed to plan for the possible loss of their partner. They worried that if their partner died, major items like their home, car, savings accounts, and investment funds might be tied up in court. They took action to relieve this worry the following ways:

- Make sure each person had their own credit cards
- Putting all major items like the home and car in both names
- Putting all bank accounts in both names or naming the partner as beneficiary
- Seeking legal consultation on financial matters for the protection of both partners
- Naming the partner as beneficiary on insurance policies and individual accounts
- Drawing up a will in consultation with an attorney

Is there any action you need to take to protect you financial assets or the financial assets of your partner in case one of you dies?

____ Yes

____ No

If so, what is it?

_____

_____

When are you going to do it?

_____

The Worst of Times

Many people control worry by planning ahead for the "worst of times." Financially, the worst of times for most people would be when

- You are without funds for the foreseeable future

- You don't have enough assets to meet your liabilities for the short- and long-term

- You have lost the ability to earn money and have depleted your resources

- You are bankrupt

If you worry about becoming destitute, you could take some of the following actions to control this worry:

- Do some research to find out what monies—such as unemployment, workers' compensation, Social Security, Social Security Disability, Welfare, housing subsidies, fuel assistance, Medicaid, Medicare, or food stamps—would be available to you in specific circumstances. Take this a step further by asking a close friend or relative to make sure you get the services you need in case your circumstances prevent you from doing this for yourself. In addition, if this is causing you a lot of worry, check out the services for the homeless in your area, such as shelters and food banks. Keep a file of this information available for easy access.

- Ask yourself, "Is there anyone who could provide me with minimal support through a hard time, even if the hard time promises to go on for a long time?" For instance, my son has told me he would support me and take care of me if I could no longer do this for myself. Maintain strong connections with family and friends. They may be your lifesavers.

- Set up savings accounts, disability insurance, and other insurance policies that would provide you with funds during difficult times.

Do you feel you need to do some advance planning to control worry about the possibility of becoming destitute?

_____ Yes

_____ No

If so, what could you do?

_____

_____

Are you going to do it?

_____ Yes

_____ No

If so, when?

_____

_____

13

Health Issues

Health and well-being—when you don't have them—can be a major cause of worry. If you can't function on a certain level, then everything becomes hard to cope with. It's all fear. And all grist for the mill. Illness and suffering changes you, your outlook and approach to life. My health was really bad at one point, so that has influenced me. Perhaps I worry less because things aren't so bad now in comparison, but I do worry because I know how bad it can be to have health problems.

The state of their health is a constant worry for many people, one that tends to change and, sometimes, intensify, with age. The downside is almost everyone seems to worry excessively about their health; the upside is there is a lot you can do about it. Gone are the days when we expected our physician to know the answers to all of our health problems. Today we know that the state of our health may depend on us. What can you do to control worry about health issues?

Educate Yourself

The number one technique cited by people in the study as a way to address and relieve health worries is to educate yourself. While it may take some research, effort, and time to find the answers you are looking for, the sources of available information are expanding rapidly. They include

- Libraries

- Bookstores

- Resource books

- The internet/world wide web (You can "bookmark" sites on the internet that you have found to be most valuable so you can easily access them again. Download articles of most interest in case they are removed before your return.)

- 800, 888, and 900 informational numbers

- Health-focused newsletters and magazines

- Classes, courses, workshops, and seminars

- Support groups

- Healthcare professionals

As part of the process of educating yourself, develop a healthcare file so you have quick access to pertinent information when you need it. It can be in a standard file cabinet or drawer, but a milk crate or a sturdy cardboard box can work just as well. File folders facilitate easy access of specific information. Your file should include:

- Health-related information you have compiled

- Copies of articles and information you have downloaded from the internet

- Copies of your health records (which belong to you and must be given to you by your physician) and all test results

- Back issues of related magazines and newsletters.

The following story from my own life illustrates the importance of educating yourself about all aspects of health-related issues:

In 1976, I went to a doctor for the first time to address the issue of my recurring deep depressions. The doctor diagnosed my depression and put me on a medication that I took daily, without fail, for ten years. I didn't really know what the medication did, what it could do to my body, when I should and shouldn't take it, or anything else that was necessary to keep me from inadvertently harming myself. My lack of education was eventually my downfall. I continued to take my medication when I had a stomach bug that had dehydrated my body. My body, without fluids, received a toxic overload, which, if it had not been treated immediately, could have been fatal.

When any health problem comes up for me now, I begin a research project. If I'm too sick to do it, a family member or friend is often willing to undertake the task. The internet has become a valuable resource for me in this process. Before I take any medication, I learn about it. I look it up in consumer-friendly books about medications and in the most current *Physicians' Desk Reference*. Sometimes, once I've read about a medication, I decide not to take it. If I do take it, I do it with appropriate respect for what it can and can't do, and how I need to manage it.

If you are considering taking a medication, the following form will help you learn all you can about any recommended medications, so you won't get into the same kind of trouble I did. You can make copies of this form to have available whenever you are considering taking a medication.

Questions to Ask the Doctor about Medication

Generic name: _____

Product name: _____

Product category: _____

Suggested dosage level: _____

How does this medication work? What do you expect it to do?

_____

_____

_____

How long will it take to achieve that result? _____

What are the risks associated with taking this medication?

_____

_____

_____

What kind of an effectiveness track record does this medication have?

_____

What short-term side effects does this medication have and how long will they last?

_____

_____

_____

What long-term side effects does this medication have?

_____

_____

_____

Is there any way to minimize the chances of experiencing these side effects?

_____ Yes

_____ No

If so, how?

_____

_____

_____

Are there any dietary or lifestyle suggestions or restrictions to be followed when using this medication?

_____

_____

_____

Why do you recommend this particular medication?

_____

_____

_____

Have you had other patients that have used it?

_____ Yes

_____ No

If so, has it worked for them?

_____

_____

_____

How is this medication monitored?

_____

_____

_____

What tests will I need prior to taking this medication?

_____

_____

_____

How often will I need these tests while taking the medication?

_____

_____

What symptoms indicate that the dosage should be changed or the medication stopped?

_____

_____

_____

Where can I get more information about this medication?

_____

_____

Do you have any printed information on this medication I can have to study?

_____ Yes

_____ No

Seek Professional Help and Support

A general healthcare practitioner who knows you and your life circumstances can assist you in monitoring your health by giving you advice on treatment, providing treatment, and referring you to other healthcare providers when necessary. One study participant said,

I try to always have a health practitioner I can turn to and ask questions, someone who knows me well, can assess my situation well, and can give good suggestions for treatment.

An annual checkup with this physician is in your best interest. Don't be satisfied with the outcome of your visit until all your questions have been answered, and you feel comfortable with the answers and with suggested treatment strategies. If necessary, arrange follow-up visits. If treatment is recommended, especially if it is serious or requires surgery, get a second opinion. Don't worry about hurting your doctor's feelings; getting a second opinion is accepted practice. If your doctor suspects you have a specific medical problem, he or she may refer you to a specialized medical professional.

In addition to getting advice, assistance, and treatment from traditional medical professionals, many people reach out to a wide variety of other healthcare practitioners for help in maintaining good health and dealing with specific health problems. The most commonly mentioned were

- **Naturopathic physicians:** healthcare professionals who specialize in a holistic treatment style including vitamin and mineral supplementation and dietary recommendations

- **Homeopathic physicians:** healthcare professionals who specialize in treatment of illness with homeopathic remedies, which are actually very minute quantities of substances that could cause symptoms similar to those you are experiencing if taken in large amounts

- **Acupuncturists:** practitioners of an Eastern form of treatment who use thin needles to stimulate various points on the body to achieve relief from symptoms

- **Chiropractors:** healthcare professionals whose focus is to help the body heal itself through spinal alignment and other noninvasive means.

Recently, complaints about lack of timely access to healthcare providers, refusal of treatment, dangerously short hospital stays, and limited choice of providers have been increasing at an alarming rate. The only way these issues can be addressed satisfactorily is if we all let our providers and elected officials know that current trends in the provision of healthcare services are not acceptable and are often dangerous.

Poor treatment from healthcare professionals can increase worry and compromise your wellness. You have a right to high quality care. You also have a right to be treated with dignity, compassion, and respect at all times. If you feel you are not getting high quality care and are not being treated well, tell your healthcare professional. If you still don't get the care and treatment you deserve, go to a different person or, if that is not possible, contact your state's Department of Protection and Advocacy (every state has such an agency) for assistance.

Diana shared the following story about a difficult healthcare situation that caused her a great deal of worry:

> Gradually I noticed that I was getting more and more tingling and feelings of numbness all over my body, which, although they weren't painful, were frightening. I contacted my doctor who was less than responsive. He said my symptoms were the result of arthritis in my neck, although I protested that I didn't have any neck pain.
>
> Over time the numbness and tingling became more intense, was increasingly accompanied by chronic muscle pain and severe muscle cramping, and I had hot, painful areas in various places on my body. I did a search on the internet and discovered that there were many possible causes of these symptoms, including multiple sclerosis. I reported this to my physician and was told in no uncertain terms that it was "all in my head." When I took a friend with me to a doctor's appointment, the doctor told me he wouldn't allow anyone else in the room while we were discussing my situation. (I found out later the doctor was totally out of order on this.) I ended my relationship with this physician and began a search for a doctor who would address my symptoms to my satisfaction.
>
> Through following up on a variety of leads, I found a good doctor who gave me an accurate diagnosis (fibromyalgia), referred me to several different specialists, and began a course of treatment. In addition I began a search for information on this little-understood condition and discovered that there were many things I could do for myself including making dietary changes and undertaking a specialized exercise regime.
>
> Now, two years later, with careful management, most of these symptoms are a thing of the past. If I had listened to my first doctor, I might have spent some time in a psychiatric hospital taking an antidepressant medication. And I would still be experiencing debilitating pain and would still be very, very worried about my future.

Filling out the following form in advance of your doctor's appointment, and giving a copy to the doctor at the time of your visit will help him or her do any detective work needed to get to the bottom of your health-related problems. Save copies of this form in your health file and have them available for subsequent visits.

Information for the Physician

1. List all medications, vitamins, and healthcare preparations you are using (or have recently used) for any reason.

Medication	Dosage	When and Why Used

2. Provide a medical history of yourself and your family.

Your history:

Mother's side of the family:

Father's side of the family:

3. Describe changes in the following categories:

Appetite or diet: _____

_____

Weight: _____

_____

Sleep patterns: _____

_____

Sex drive: _____

_____

Ability to concentrate: _____

_____

Memory: _____

_____

4. Have you recently had any of the following symptoms? (Put a check mark next to those that apply.)

_____ Headaches

    Describe: _____

    _____

_____ Numbness or tingling anywhere

    Describe: _____

    _____

_____ Loss of balance

    Describe: _____

    _____

_____ Double vision or vision problems

    Describe: _____

    _____

____ Periods of amnesia

Describe: _____

_____

____ Coordination changes

Describe: _____

_____

____ Weakness in arms or legs

Describe: _____

_____

____ Fever

Describe: _____

_____

____ Nausea or diarrhea

Describe: _____

_____

____ Other gastrointestinal problems

Describe: _____

_____

____ Fainting or dizziness

Describe: _____

_____

____ Seizures

Describe: _____

_____

____ Stressful life events

Describe: _____

_____

(You can add additional sheets for other pertinent information.)

Get Support

Worries can increase if you try to deal with health-related issues on your own. As many study participants found, close family members and friends who are validating and affirming and with whom you can discuss these issues can provide relief and diversion from worry, as well as additional practical information and advice.

> When I was having a really hard time with recurring severe headaches, my sister and several close friends made all the difference. Without them I'm not sure I would have persisted until I found relief. I was tired of visiting healthcare professionals who didn't seem to understand the effect of these headaches on my life.

> My wife has a chronic illness—fibromyalgia—that limits what she can do. I learned about the illness and try to help her when she is suffering.

> I was going into the hospital for testing and diagnosis of a frightening skin lesion. My doctor had explained the possibilities, and, frankly, I was scared. My wife went with me to the hospital and stayed with me until I got the "all clear." Then she took me home, cooked me my favorite dinner, and pampered me through the evening. It was a small gesture on her part—but it made all the difference for me.

Supporters can help by

- Accompanying you to healthcare appointments

- Providing reassurance, encouragement, information, and advice

- Seeking additional information when you can't do this for yourself

- Listening when you need someone to talk to

- Providing you with care when you can't care for yourself

Who could support you if you were trying to deal with a health problem?

How could they help?

_____

_____

_____

Often, others will not realize you need help, or, if they do realize you need help, will not know what to do. Good friends and family members are usually more than willing to provide care if they know what would be helpful. This is the time to let go of old attitudes about taking care of yourself. Ask supporters for help and then tell them exactly what you need them to do. It's so much better than having them wondering what to do. You can always return the favor when you're feeling better and they are having a hard time.

Accept Your Situation and Counter Negative Thoughts

You may have a healthcare condition that cannot be changed, or one in which the outcome is uncertain. You can spend a lot of time engrossed in useless worry about such a circumstance. Once you have done everything you can to address, treat, and make adjustments relative to the situation, it's time for letting go, accepting, or making a significant change in attitude to control your worry and make your life more comfortable and enjoyable.

Many people found affirmations such as this one helpful:

I will address these symptoms systematically, do what I can to understand and relieve them, and spend the rest of my time thinking about and doing things that make my life enjoyable.

List things you would enjoy doing rather than thinking negative thoughts about a health condition:

_____

_____

_____

Accepting your situation may not be something you can do right away, but you can begin the process by countering your negative thoughts with positive ones. Here are some examples of positive statements that can be repeated to counteract negative or detrimental thoughts or attitudes:

Negative Thought or Attitude	Positive Statement
My life is over.	*My life is different but well worth living.*
I can't deal with this.	*I'm doing the best I can to deal with this effectively.*
This will just get worse and worse.	*I'll deal with whatever happens.*
Why me?	*Difficult things happen to everyone.*
This is intolerable.	*I can live with this.*
I'll never be able to do the things I enjoy again.	*I will continue to do many of the things I enjoy.*

List health-related negative thoughts and attitudes that cause or increase your worry and positive statements that counteract them.

Negative Thought or Attitude	Positive Statement
_____	_____
_____	_____
_____	_____
_____	_____

Once you have determined positive statements that will counteract negative thoughts and attitudes, repeat them over and over when the negative thoughts and attitudes come up, when you first get up in the morning, before you go to bed at night, and anytime you have a few minutes during the day. Repeat them aloud when possible. Write them over and over. Journal about them. Write the positive statements on Post-it Notes, put them in various places around your home and read them aloud or to yourself whenever you see them. With persistence you will notice that your thoughts and attitudes become more positive and you will be worrying less.

Refer to chapter 3, "Techniques for Dealing with Worry," for more information on changing negative thoughts to positive ones and the resources listed in the back of the book.

One woman who had had surgery for a melanoma continued to worry even after everything checked out well. She realized, however, that the worry was doing her no good and that she could not predict her future; she had to accept that and go on with life. She got regular checkups, looked to the positive, and refused to stew in it. She directed her mind to live in the present and not imagine the worst.

Take Good Care of Yourself

Taking good care of yourself is the best strategy for maintaining wellness and reducing worry about health-related issues. Everyone in the study agreed that you can benefit from focusing on what you need to do to keep yourself healthy and then making a concerted effort to do these things regularly.

One study participant felt that recent changes he'd introduced into his life helped ease his worries about his health:

> I make an effort to eat well, walk six to ten miles a week, practice meditation ten minutes a day, and take a weekly yoga class. I bathe every day, wear fresh clothes, look well, and sleep at least six hours a night. I eat three meals a day. I do not eat red meat, smoke, drink alcohol, or abuse other substances.

You can develop a list for keeping track of those things you need to do on a daily basis to attain the highest level of wellness possible. Post the list in a convenient place and check it daily to make sure you are doing everything possible to keep yourself well. Following is an example of such a list:

- Eat three balanced meals.
- Eat small healthy snacks between meals.
- Drink six to eight glasses of water.
- Avoid the excessive use of sugar and processed, highly salted, or fatty foods.
- Avoid caffeine.
- Avoid smoking and secondhand smoke.
- Exercise for thirty minutes.
- Spend at least thirty minutes involved in a creative, affirming, or fun activity.
- Spend time with positive, affirming people.

In addition, you may want to ask yourself the following questions every few days:

- *Do I need to see my doctor or some other healthcare professional?*
- *Is there a symptom or health problem that I need to address?*
- *Do I need to get more rest or sleep?*
- *Would I feel better if I got a massage?*
- *Do I need some extended exercise?*

Use this space to develop your own daily maintenance list.

Daily Health Maintenance List

List those things you need to do daily to stay well.

- _____
- _____
- _____
- _____
- _____
- _____
- _____
- _____

Get Rid of Habits That Are Detrimental to Good Health

Numerous study participants felt that they could let go of worries about health-related issues if they gave up some bad habits that compromise their chances for long-term wellness. The three top concerns were smoking, substance abuse, and poor eating habits (eating too much, too little, or the wrong things).

Study participants reported the following:

I have ten-plus years of nondrinking with the help of AA and nine years of nonsmoking due to a hospital program. Both programs worked, but it was not an easy process. I would like to do the same for food but am having a hard time.

I try not to think about this, but the truth is that I'm concerned about being too heavy. I've tried a zillion things from diets to hypnosis. I'd like to eat a healthy way and not think about weight, but I'm a food addict.

Weight, appearance, and addictions all go together for me. If I could *control* the amount I eat, I could *lose weight* and I would *look and feel better.*

I have taken a "life steps" course at a hospital to lose twenty-five pounds. It worked for a while. I wish I could lose weight for self-image as well as health. I need to make it a high priority and exercise self-control with food.

Here are some strategies that have worked for others to help change unhealthy habits:

Twelve-Step Programs

While best known for their success in helping people let go of an addiction to alcohol, these are now being used to successfully address other addictions. Your local Yellow Pages, as well as some newspapers, will have a listing of such groups in your area.

Support Groups

There are numerous support groups available that are designed to help individuals give up specific addictions. Support from others who are trying to let go of a similar habit is very valuable. In addition, support groups can be a source of good information, new ideas, and even new supporters. These groups may be sponsored by hospitals, health maintenance organizations, or mental health centers and are often free of charge.

Keeping Written Records of Goals and Progress

Many people find that developing short-term goals (many people in the study referred to these as "baby steps") and keeping a daily record of progress is a valuable tool in letting go of an addictive habit. A simple spiral notebook works well. You can use a form like the one that follows, or develop a form of your own. This form is for smoking but it can be modified for any addiction.

Smoking Reduction Record

Date: _____ Goal for the day: _____

Morning:

_____ # of cigarettes smoked

_____ # less than previous day

Diversionary strategies that helped:

_____

_____

_____

How I felt:

_____

_____

Afternoon:

____ # of cigarettes smoked

____ # less than previous day

Diversionary strategies that helped

_____

_____

_____

How I felt:

_____

_____

Evening:

____ # of cigarettes smoked

____ # less than previous day

Diversionary strategies that helped

_____

_____

_____

How I felt:

_____

_____

Goal for tomorrow:

_____

_____

When you have achieved your daily goals for a length of time determined by you, for instance one week with half as many cigarettes as when you began, or two weeks with no sweet snacks, reward yourself by doing something you enjoy or buying yourself something special you have been wanting.

A food record should include a listing of everything you ate, how much you ate, when you ate it, why you ate it, and how you felt when you ate it. This record could also include how much exercise you've gotten.

One woman reported that she was having little success losing the fifteen pounds her doctor recommended as part of a prescription for overall wellness. She knew that the extra weight was decreasing her energy and contributing to ongoing pain in her knees and hips but still couldn't stick to a diet. She began keeping daily records of everything she ate. After she recorded what she ate for a week she used the information to set up short-term goals to guide her along her journey. When she reviewed her findings she realized for the first time that she was eating more food than she thought she was. She hadn't taken into account the nibble here and the nibble there. This realization got her on the right track and she is slowly but consistently losing the weight.

Working Closely with a Specialist

There are numerous healthcare professionals and counselors who work specifically with people who are trying to give up addictions or change poor health habits. They can advise you on the strategies and treatments that would work best for you. They can also provide you with the support that is needed to accomplish this difficult task. They have often dealt with a similar issue in their own lives. Your health insurance company or health management organization may be willing to refer you to such a specialist and cover some or all of the costs.

Self-Help Books

Self-help books can guide you through the process of breaking addictive habits. The resources section in the back of the book lists some of them.

Visualization Exercises

Visualization exercises like those described in chapter 4, "Focusing Your Attention Away from Worry," or in the book *Visualization for Change* (Fanning 1994) can be effective aids in helping you get rid of bad habits. The following examples can serve as a guide in developing your own visualization sequences. Use your creative senses to develop an exercise that will work for you.

In *Visualization for Change*, Patrick Fanning describes a visualization exercise that you could use if you want to lose weight and develop healthy eating habits. It begins by lying down and making yourself comfortable. You then imagine yourself going through the day in great detail, enjoying the way your body looks at the desired weight, wearing attractive, new, smaller clothes, making healthy food choices, savoring the tastes of these foods, enjoying exercising, and walking with yourself through the times when you are tempted to eat the wrong foods or overeat. You could do parts of this visualization at different times of the day to help you get through difficult times.

Visualization exercises to help you give up smoking can be repeated frequently during the day. Fanning says the nonsmoking visualization needs three elements:

1. An example of successfully getting your needs met without smoking

2. An image of yourself as a healthy nonsmoker

3. An image of smoking as unpleasant—like the smell of cigarette smoke making you queasy

Substitute a Healthy Habit for the Unhealthy Habit

In order to do this, you must first make a list of the reasons you engage in this habit. For example, I eat

- To feel happy

- To nurture myself

- Because I like the taste of food

- To relieve stress

Make your own list of reasons why you engage in _____ (bad habit):

- _____

- _____

- _____

- _____

- _____

Making this list will guide you in thinking of other things you could do that meet the same need but are not bad for you, and may even be good for you. Then you can make a list of these things. For example, instead of grabbing something unhealthy to eat, I could

- Call a friend

- Write a card to someone I care about

- Go for a walk

- Take a few deep breaths

- Write about the feelings in my journal

- Work on a knitting project

- Weed in the garden

- Make myself some tea

- Read a book

- Eat a piece of fruit

List some things you could do instead of _____ (bad habit):

- _____

- _____

- _____

- _____

- _____

Taking "Baby Steps"

Getting rid of a bad habit that has persisted for years, perhaps most of your life, can feel like a daunting task. Because it seems so overwhelming, the tendency is to put it off until just the right time—when you're not so busy, when you've gotten the house cleaned, when you've finished writing your doctoral thesis, after the kids are all through college. Actually there is no better time to do it than right now. The sooner you meet your goal, whether it is losing sixty pounds, gaining fifteen pounds, giving up alcohol, or avoiding gambling, the sooner you will be enjoying a renewed sense of health and well-being.

Not long ago, I weighed twenty pounds more than I needed to, which was making it difficult to recover from a chronic muscular pain condition. I decided to set reasonable monthly goals for myself—four pounds a month (or one pound a week). When I met my monthly goal, I bought myself a piece of clothing as a treat—a silly pair of socks or an attractive scarf. When I met my goal of twenty pounds, I bought a soft Polartec jacket that I had been coveting. The greatest reward, however, has been diminished chronic pain. I can now cross-country ski, bicycle, and hike—all activities I was afraid I would have to give up.

Hypnosis

Study participants reported that they had let go of bad habits by seeing a trained hypnotist or through self-hypnosis. If seeing a trained hypnotist feels right to you, get recommendations from others who have used the services of a hypnotist. Make sure the hypnotist is specially trained. There are many self-help books that teach self-hypnosis. They can show you how to guide yourself into a trance and then repeat powerful statements that will create positive changes in the way you think and the things you do. I recommend *Hypnosis for Change* (Hadley and Staudacher 1996).

A man in the study had been smoking since he was in his teens. Now, in his late thirties, he was acutely aware of the effects this habit was having on every aspect of his life. His skin was dry and taut. His teeth had yellowed. He was noticing some shortness of breath. His clothes smelled of cigarette smoke, and he noticed yellow stains around the ceiling in his apartment. He decided to go to a hypnotist. The hypnotist discussed with him why he smoked, what need it filled in his life, and why he wanted to let go of it. Then the hypnotist led him into a hypnotic state of which he has no memory. That was seven years ago. He has had no desire for a cigarette since that time.

Create an Emergency Plan

Some people relieve worry about possible short- or long-term health emergencies by developing an emergency plan that give supporters directions on how they want to be treated and cared for in the event they lose the ability to make these decisions for themselves.

I have had recurring episodes of severe, suicidal depression in the past. When I was well I realized that, by not having an emergency plan for my supporters, I was putting my health and life at risk. Although it was hard to think of the possibility of experiencing such deep despair again, I felt it was in my best interest, and in the best interest of my family and friends to develop for them a set of instructions to use as a guide in case I got very depressed again. It has helped control worry for everyone involved.

Following is an example of an emergency plan:

Emergency Plan

Name: _____ Date: _____

Symptoms or circumstances that indicate to others that they need to take over full responsibility for my care and make decisions in my behalf:

- I don't know my family members and friends.
- I can't do the things I normally do to take care of myself and my family.
- I do not respond to others.
- I am unable to get out of bed.

If the above symptoms or circumstances come up, I want the following people to take over for me:

Name	Connection/Role	Phone Number
Amelia Jones	Sister	555-4637
Tammy Searles	Best friend	555-7683
Edward Frank	Spouse	555-4273

| Dr. Harriette Shipp | Physician | 555-4932 |
| Laura Ellis | Nurse practitioner | 555-4932 |

I *do not* want the following people involved in any way in my care or treatment:

| **Name** | **Why I Do Not Want Them Involved (optional)** |
| Dr. Thomas Jones | Uncomfortable with his style |

If my supporters disagree on what is to be done, I want my spouse to make the final decision.

Medications I am currently using and why I am taking them:

- Synthroid in the morning for hypothyroidism
- Multivitamin in the morning

Medications that would be acceptable to me if medications became necessary and why or when I would choose those:

- Darvon for pain
- Tagamet for ulcers

Medications that should be avoided and why:

- Steroids have given me severe side effects in the past.

Treatments that have helped me in the past and when they should be used:

- A massage always helps me feel better.
- If my breast cancer recurs, chemotherapy is acceptable.

Treatments I would want to avoid:

- I do not want any experimental treatments.

If possible I would like to stay at home and be cared for by family members and friends who take turns providing my care. If hospitalization becomes necessary, I prefer these treatment facilities:

- Vermont General Hospital
- Franklin Health Center

Treatment facilities I want to avoid:

- Country Convalescent Home
- Tamworth Community Hospital

Things that others can do for me that would help me feel better:

- Play me music from my compact disc collection
- Give me a back rub
- Read to me from the poetry books on the shelf by my bed
- Serve me healthy, wholesome foods with no dairy or sugar
- Hug me
- Tell me what is going on

Things I need others to do for me and who I want to do what:

What I Need Done	Who I'd Like to Do It
Pay my bills	My son Tom
Keep the house clean, water my plants, buy the groceries	My sister Susan
Take care of the pets	My daughter Patti
Pick up and sort the mail	My friend Sue

Things that others might do, or have done in the past, that would not help or might even make the situation worse:

- Force me to do things
- Chatter incessantly
- Play rock music

I developed this plan on _____ (date) with the help of Edward Frank.

Any plan with a more recent date supersedes this one.

Signed _____ Date _____

Witness _____ Date _____

Witness _____ Date _____

Attorney (optional) _____ Date _____

You can use the following form to develop your emergency plan. Once you have developed an emergency plan, give copies to all the people who would be involved in your care. Keep one copy in your file and let others know where to find it. Update the form as your condition changes. If you have access to a computer, keeping this form on a disk can ease the process of making changes.

Emergency Plan

Name: _____ Date: _____

Symptoms or circumstances that indicate to others that they need to take over full responsibility for my care and make decisions in my behalf:

- _____

- _____

- _____

- _____

- _____

If the above symptoms or circumstances come up, I want the following people to take over for me:

Name	Connection/Role	Phone number
_____	_____	_____
_____	_____	_____
_____	_____	_____
_____	_____	_____
_____	_____	_____

I *do not* want the following people involved in any way in my care or treatment:

Name	Why I do not want them involved (optional)
_____	_____
_____	_____
_____	_____
_____	_____

If my supporters disagree on what is to be done, I want _____ to make the final decision.

Medications I am currently using and why I am taking them:

- _____

- _____

- _____
- _____

Medications that would be acceptable to me if medications became necessary and why or when I would choose those:

- _____
- _____
- _____
- _____

Medications that should be avoided and why:

- _____
- _____
- _____
- _____

Treatments that have helped me in the past and when they should be used:

- _____
- _____
- _____
- _____

Treatments I would want to avoid:

- _____
- _____
- _____
- _____

Plan so that I can stay at home or in the community and still get the care I need:

- _____
- _____
- _____
- _____
- _____

Treatment facilities where I prefer to be treated or hospitalized if that becomes necessary:

- _____
- _____
- _____
- _____

Treatment facilities I want to avoid:

- _____
- _____
- _____
- _____

Things that others can do for me that would help me feel better:

- _____
- _____
- _____
- _____
- _____
- _____

Things I need others to do for me and who I want to do what:

What I Need Done	Who I'd Like to Do It
_____	_____
_____	_____
_____	_____
_____	_____
_____	_____

Things that others might do, or have done in the past, that would not help or might even make the situation worse:

- _____
- _____

- _____
- _____
- _____
- _____

I developed this plan on _____ (date) with the help of _____ .

Any plan with a more recent date supersedes this one.

Signed _____   Date _____

Witness _____   Date _____

Witness _____   Date _____

Attorney (optional) _____   Date _____

Take Precautions

Worry can be relieved by taking precautions that protect you from some chronic and acute illnesses. Some prudent guidelines that are in everyone's best interest include the following:

- Wash your hands with soap before meals, after toileting, and at regular intervals throughout the day.
- Take echinacea (an herbal immune system booster) before being in crowded or confined spaces.
- Maintain adequate fluid intake.
- Keep life stress at a manageable level.
- Limit the intake of sugar, salt, and fats.
- Eat plenty of fresh fruits and vegetables.
- Take multivitamin preparations with extra vitamins E and C.
- Assess personal or genetic risk factors and take steps to minimize the susceptibility to these factors.
- For women, do monthly breasts exams and have mammograms at intervals recommended by your physician.
- For men, have regular prostate examinations.
- Wear protective clothing when in natural areas where poison ivy or oak, snake bites, insects, or ticks might be a problem. Inspect your body for ticks after being outdoors.

Since AIDS became a major health hazard in the early 1980s, there are health precautions that need to be taken by anyone in a vulnerable position:

- Avoid contact with the body fluids of others. If you work in a job where this is not possible, wear latex gloves and goggles or mask if needed.

- Avoid using intravenous needles that have been used by others.

- Use a condom or other barrier type protection when having sex if you are not in a monogamous relationship, or if you or your partner have had other sexual partners since being tested for AIDS and other sexually transmitted diseases.

Relieve worry about AIDS by getting an HIV test through your physician or anonymous testing by a local health agency or AIDS project.

14

Relationship Issues

Relationships have always been a major source of worry for me.
I am a "people person" and my relationships with others affect
every aspect of my life. When I feel "out of sync" in any of my
relationships—with my kids, my partner, my parents, my
friends, my colleagues at work—I worry about it incessantly.

Worries related to relationships can involve many issues—being single, married, or in a committed relationship; being part of a family; being a single parent; or being a good friend.

Being Single

People in the study who fell into the category of single include those who had never been in an intimate relationship, those who had been in a relationship that had ended, and those who were divorced and widowed.

Some of these people are content with their single status:

> I'm single and free! I have less worry at this point. I enjoy my freedom and have a deeper connection to friends.

> I'm divorced. I enjoy being single! By staying single I have good friends, both women and men. I am not eager to remarry although I

have had opportunities to do so. My kids love me and are helpful and supportive.

I am enjoying the solitude after a four-year, intense (and very satisfying) relationship.

Some people felt okay with being along, for the time being, but didn't necessarily rule out the possibility of a relationship:

Sometimes I wish I had a live-in companion to ease my responsibilities, but that's not always easy either. I have a good life and love my solitude. Everything changes though and maybe that will too, someday.

When alone, I worry about being alone, about the relationship I lost, and about whether I'm going to have a good relationship in the future. With a partner, I worry about the relationship and I worry about me.

I may or may not have another partner. But no matter what happens, I am making sure that my life is rich and full, setting up a lifestyle I enjoy whether or not I ever get into an intimate relationship.

Many people said emphatically that they didn't like being alone. One man, whose partner of twenty years died suddenly, said,

I don't like being alone. I don't need a lot of people around, but the world doesn't seem real if I don't have someone to share it with. I became very introverted and started drinking a lot more, after John died. He and I had been together since I was in college. I was scared to be alone in the house. It seemed like it was way too much to handle. So I developed a routine. I'd come home, have a six-pack of beer, and then go to bed. I never did anything. I was very mad at my partner for leaving me. I wanted to sit in the backyard with a keg of beer and drink until I died. When I finally stopped drinking and began going to AA, my life changed. But I still don't feel like a real person when I don't have someone to share it with.

Others, too, expressed pain in being alone:

Even though I have very caring adult children, I sometimes feel that nobody really cares about me and my well being.

I worry about finding a partner—will I ever? I worry about having children. I worry about financial security, growing old alone, and what others think of me being single. However, I don't think being single makes me worry more. I believe it just makes me worry about different things. I try not to focus on it and have faith that I will find a life partner and that my worries will be alleviated.

I am single, and single is lonely. Loving someone and being loved by them is conducive to calmness, peace, and happiness. At some point in the future, I will be with someone I love and who loves me.

If you are single, how do you feel about it?

_____

_____

_____

Do you want to be in a relationship?

_____ Yes

_____ No

How do you feel that being in a relationship would affect your worry?

_____

_____

_____

Understandably, wanting to be in a relationship and wondering if you will ever be in one is a key worry of many people who are single. Following are some ways people in the study found partners:

- Go to community activities.
- Start a group (support group, book group, walking group, and so on).
- Join a group.
- Place a personals ad or respond to one.
- Contact a dating service.
- Volunteer at an organization that interests you.
- Join a men's or women's social network.
- Join a network of people with similar interests.
- Network with friends.

Many people spoke of cultivating relationships that are not necessarily romantic. Good friendships, too, can alleviate loneliness.

I have joined or initiated groups where I can feel a sense of mutual support. I've taken the initiative in getting to know new friends who appeal to me.

I definitely worry that I will always be alone. But I don't really worry about it socially. I have built up strong friendships, hang out with friends on weekends, and have lots of people to talk to when the fears and doubts arise.

The following worries and possible solutions were shared by single people in the study:

Issues That Cause Worry	Possible Solutions
Whether or not you want to be in a relationship	Get clarity by journaling, talking to friends, and peer counseling.
Feeling that something is wrong with you	Work on building your self-esteem. Ask trusted supporters if there is something you are doing that is turning others off and, if so, work to change it.
There'll be no one to take care of you when you get older	Do some advance planning to assure that you will be taken care of when you grow old.
Never having children	Explore options for having children that are independent of whether you are in a relationship.
Supporting yourself	See chapter 12, "Financial Worries."
Something might happen to you and know one will know	Arrange with neighbors and friends to check in with you regularly.
Getting over the loss of your partner	Attend grief support groups. Peer counsel. Attend community events or meetings of special interest groups. Arrange time to get together with friends and family members daily, and at those times when you feel worse, such as on weekends and holidays. Keep yourself busy doing things you enjoy. Develop new interests and activities.

If you are single and have worries (about being single) that you wish to control or relieve, use the following space to write your worries, possible solutions, and a plan of action. Use ideas in this section, from other chapters of the book, and other solutions you have discovered.

Worry: _____

Possible solution: _____

_____

When are you going to take this action?

_____

How are going to do it?

_____

_____

_____

Worry: _____

Possible solution: _____

_____

When are you going to take this action?

_____

How are going to do it?

_____

_____

_____

Worry: _____

Possible solution: _____

_____

When are you going to take this action?

_____

How are going to do it?

_____

_____

_____

Single Parenting

Raising a child or children on your own brings with it its own set of worries, whether single parenting is an option you chose, was the result of a failed relationship, or came about because of the death of a partner.

A widower and father of two children, ages six and eight, said,

> I really love my kids. They are my life. But since the unexpected death of my wife, the going has been tough. I think I took over her role as the parent who worries about the kids.

A woman who chose to adopt two children from South American countries as infants (they are now ages eight and thirteen) said,

> This choice was a good one. My kids have really enriched my life. But sometimes I just wish I had someone to help out, to share the load. And I worry that the kids don't have a father figure in their lives. My Dad tries to do the best he can but he's older and doesn't live in the area.

Another woman has always been a single parent, although her thirteen-year-old son's father has occasionally contributed to parenting. She has been in a number of semi-committed relationships, but finds that being a single parent can really affect a romantic relationship.

> Being a single parent makes for a lot of worries. Does my lover care for my son? (And vice versa.) Will the relationship last? *Should* it last? I have tried therapy, talking about it, analyzing it, trying to bulldoze through, and burying things. In the past, I have left some relationships when it wasn't working with my son.

Through creative problem solving many single parents have relieved their worries and are, as a result, finding their role to be much more enjoyable. Following are some common issues that cause worry for single parents along with some possible solutions.

Issues That Cause Worry	Possible Solutions
Childcare	Network with others in similar situations to find appropriate providers. Set up a cooperative childcare situation with other parents who have similar needs. Exchange childcare with friends who are also parents. Find employment in a business that has a daycare center.

	Take the children along to work whenever possible.
	Interview childcare providers in advance to increase your comfort level.
	Have a cooperative rather than an adversarial, relationship with childcare providers.
	Work at home.
Health of children and self	Make regular appointments with healthcare professionals rather than on an "as needed" basis.
	Research and read about healthcare and take appropriate preventive action.
	Focus on a healthy diet.
	Supplement children's food with vitamins and minerals.
	See chapter 13, "Health Issues."
Money: making ends meet	See chapter 12, "Financial Worries."
	Use welfare supports when necessary.
	Ask family and/or friends for help.
How children are doing in school	Meet regularly with your children's teachers.
	Attend school functions.
	Volunteer at your children's school.
	Tutor at home.
	Make educational resources available at home.
Lack of personal support with raising children	Arrange time to collaborate with others in similar situations.
	Join or start a support group.
Lack of time	Restrict your activities to those that are most life enriching to you and your children.
	Avoid overcommitment.
	Involve your children in your work and play when appropriate.
Whether or not someone will think you are a bad parent	Practice letting go of what others think and do the best you can.

Issues That Cause Worry	Possible Solutions
Whether or not someone will take the kids away	Practice being in the moment. Spend quality time with your children. Make your children your highest priority. Have plans set up for the care of your children in the event that you become unable to provide them with care.
Whether or not you should have stayed with the other parent for the sake of the kids	Get involved in counseling or peer counseling.
Finding another partner in spite of the fact that you have kids	Get involved in counseling. Repeat affirmations. Attend a support group for single parents. Make time for your own social life and activities.
Whether or not a new partner treats the children well; will they get along with each other?	Get involved in counseling. Engage in mutual support and dialoguing. Read books on the subject.

If you are a single parent and have worries that you wish to control or relieve, use the following space to write your worries, possible solutions, and a plan of action. Use ideas in this section, from other chapters of the book, and other solutions you have discovered.

Worry: _____

Possible solution: _____

_____

When are you going to take this action?

_____

How are going to do it?

_____

_____

_____

Worry: _____

Possible solution: _____

_____

When are you going to take this action?

_____

How are going to do it?

_____

_____

_____

Worry: _____

Possible solution: _____

_____

When are you going to take this action?

_____

How are going to do it?

_____

_____

_____

Partnered or Married

While being in a committed relationship is often touted as the ideal, it comes with its own worries. The diversity of responses to study questions shows the variety of worries one encounters in a close relationship and the creativity people have used, sometimes more successfully than others, in addressing these concerns.

Consider the following quotes from "partnered" study participants addressing their worries:

> I am in a long-term, committed relationship. My relationship is flawed, and I sometimes wish it were more ideal. I have tried to get my companion to change his behaviors that bother me but have not generally been successful at this.

Without the bumps, it would be perfect. But with the bumps, it seems almost more enduring and therefore secure. We've done the vomit-up-your-brains-and-delve-deeply-into-this-relationship, the marriage counseling, the separation, and now we are trying sailing therapy and it is the best yet. A great book that helped is *Marriage Shock*, by Dalma Heyn. It talks about how having fun and being your fun self, true self, beats trying to be the wifely icon.

I still get fear of abandonment. I have become very dependent on the relationship. I know I am a better person in a relationship. The whole is much bigger than the two halves.

Ten years with him has made me more secure and more able to cope with things. I know I could cope if anything happened. Hurts from childhood have faded in this conducive and warm environment. We have developed so many friends and such a strong support group. My partner would have a lot of support if anything happened to me as well, so I feel more comfortable with that. Our lives have blossomed

I worry about how my partner will react to certain things and whether the relationship will endure. In the past I dealt with this by stuffing my feelings and feeling bad. More recently I have dealt with this by confronting the problems and my partner as things come up. I have realized that all I can control is my own feelings and behaviors.

My husband and I have been married for twenty-eight years and have experienced many ups and downs. Our relationship is a good one but we definitely give each other training. Over the years there have been some worrisome times when it looked like we were not going to make it. We did counseling several times.

Having a partner to share concerns with reduces the intensity of my concerns and lessens the opportunity to become worried. During my midthirties, I worried a lot about being unloved, undesirable, and abandoned and lonely. I feel more secure now. I love myself more. I enjoy having my spouse, but I am less fearful of loss.

I worry less about financial security and more about if my husband's activities are working opposite to what I'm trying to do. I've accepted that we can be very different in many respects and still have a good relationship. I've become better at verbal communication and listening. I accept that there are reasons for us to be together, and we are learning from each other's differences.

Being married to my #1 supporter makes my life a lot easier than it would otherwise be. I don't worry about divorce, but I do worry about something happening to him when he travels. We work on our issues by talking things through and occasionally arguing a little bit. Before we got married we went for some joint counseling. I have more of a need to talk about things than he does, so I find other people to talk to about my concerns, including my therapist.

I am thrilled to be in a great relationship (monogamous). I do not have to worry about contracting HIV, I do not have to go it alone, I have someone concerned. I'm proud a gay couple is visible—out. I am thrilled about that. My partner is twenty-two years older than I am, and I have some concern that I may live twenty-two years without him. There are no certainties. I try to have a positive impact on his weight/diet and exercise so he will be healthier and live longer.

Being in a relationship helps because my partner is *not* a worrier, and he's able to laugh at me/with me. Sometimes it makes it harder because he's unaware of lots of the day-to-day little things. I let him shake me out of it with his laughter and try to let go of some of the things. I talk to him about some of my worries and ask for help to problem solve.

Mostly I have learned to set aside attempting to take responsibility for my partner's satisfaction with his life. The more compassionate I am towards myself, the more able I am to forgive my partner, while at the same time staying clear of the impossible task of trying to live his life for him.

I am drawn to being in relationship, but I am so claustrophobic when I am partnered. I've tried lots of things. I wish I could just stop worrying—either be with the relationship or out of it, not in halfway and worrying. I don't know how to make that happen. I wonder if I should just be alone.

Clearly there are many worries for people in committed relationships. Some of them are about real situations. Others are about problems that might come up. How do people in the study say they address and resolve these worries?

Issues That Cause Worry	Possible Solutions
Partner's health problems	Encourage and support your partner in healthy living and share health concerns.

	Get help and support if necessary in providing care. Join a support group for caregivers if appropriate. Take good care of yourself.
Acceptance of partner by family	Arrange pleasant, comfortable family gatherings so people can get to know each other in a relaxed atmosphere.
Differences in values	Adopt an attitude of acceptance of differences rather than trying to change them. Discuss the positive in each different value system. Go to couples therapy.
Difficulty communicating	Go to couples therapy. Set aside time to talk and listen to each other without giving advice, criticism, or judgment.
Differences in sex drive	Engage in open discussion. Go to couples therapy. Get a physical examination and discuss the issue with physician. Look in resource books.
Jealousy	Have open communication. Go to individual or couples therapy.
One partner wanting more commitment than the other	Have open communication. Compromise within reason. Go to counseling.
The state of the relationship	Doing everything you can to keep the relationship healthy and vibrant, and keep yourself healthy and vibrant—for your *own* sake.
Fear of losing your partner	Since there are never any guarantees in life, develop a strong sense of self and a variety of personal interests and activities to carry you through in case this loss occurs. Assure yourself that you can make it on your own.

Issues That Cause Worry	Possible Solutions
	Have a back-up life plan that you will use in case you are alone.
	Have joint ownership of major items, like the home and car, so neither partner is left without access to these things.
	Have wills, insurance policies, and other funds that provide for each other.
If one of you changes and the other doesn't	Collaborate on how to incorporate these changes into the relationship.
Fear of becoming unattractive to your partner	Take good care of yourself. Share mutual interests.
Infidelity	Go to couples therapy.
Anger or resentment	Go to couples therapy. Discuss the issue to resolve differences. Apologize and/or take action if appropriate.
If your partner is or becomes abusive	Go to individual or couples therapy. Contact the local crisis services. Do whatever is necessary to keep yourself from being abused, including leaving.

Reading some of the many books on relationships can be a powerful tool for some people, especially if both partners read and agree with the same book. There are more and more relationship workshops being offered as well, some devoted to problem solving and some to growth. Check with your local counseling agency, church group, or metropolitan newspaper advertisements.

My relationship is very important to me and I am willing to put a lot of time and energy into keeping it strong and healthy. Study participants agreed that the following strategies are essential to keeping relationships healthy and controlling worry:

- Regular, open communication

- Setting aside time for "dates"—movies, dining out, dancing, and so on

- Regular, creative sex in usual and unusual places

- Enjoying silence together

- Working and playing together—keeping a balance
- Sharing humor, joy, sadness, and dessert
- Sharing mutual tasks
- Trading compliments
- Focusing on what you love about each other
- Giving each other plenty of space to be who you are
- Going to bed at the same time at least several times a week
- Practicing unconditional acceptance and love

If you are in a committed relationship and you have worries about being in this relationship that you wish to control or relieve, use the following space to write your worries, possible solutions, and a plan of action. Use ideas in this section, from other chapters of the book, and other solutions you have discovered.

Worry: _____

Possible solution: _____

_____

When are you going to take this action?

_____

How are going to do it?

_____

_____

_____

Worry: _____

Possible solution: _____

_____

When are you going to take this action?

_____

How are going to do it?

_____

_____

_____

Worry: _____

Possible solution: _____

_____

When are you going to take this action?

_____

How are going to do it?

_____

_____

_____

Family Relations

Family life is at best rich and rewarding, something most people treasure. Family worries can be complex, involving several people, yet they are perhaps easier to address than, say, global concerns.

Your Children

I wouldn't trade my history with a growing family for anything, but I don't think I ever worried more than when my children were growing up. Study participants had a great deal to say about worries related to children:

> I'm down to one weathered husband, one teenaged daughter, and two great cats. The only worries have to do with division of labor about cleaning and cooking. I bitch, it works for one day max, and then everything falls back to baseline. I've just begun to work outside the home full-time, so change is in order here and hopefully will be forthcoming.

> It can be hard for me to share my space with other people, even my children. But the good part is that I don't have to do everything myself, and I have a sense of family. We resolve worries by talking and letting each other know what we need. It also helps to create structures—a regular time for cleaning, bedtime rituals, and together-versus-apart times.

> I have a five-year-old son and a baby on the way. It means there are lots of details to worry about. There are also lots of joys, and my son takes me away from my worrying when I let him, which is fairly often—unless there are very heavy stresses in our lives.

I live with my husband, a thirteen-year-old son, and a six-year-old daughter. I worry about having the time, space, and quiet to do things that are meaningful or rejuvenating for me personally.

Undoubtedly there are more opportunities for worry in busy family life. However, the physical time available for worry is not there, so "worrying" is never a priority.

As situations occur, I talk it over with individual family members, sometimes in the context of the entire family. In very serious situations, I seek the help of a professional, that is, teacher, counselor, pastor.

The following issues that cause worry about children and family life and possible solutions to these worries were shared by study participants:

Issues That Cause Worry	Possible Solutions
Division of labor: who's going to do what	Develop "chore charts" or other systems so family members know what they have to do and when. Have family meetings to discuss who is going to do what. Give rewards (money or other agreed upon treats).
Health and safety of family members	Take appropriate preventive health and safety measures.
All the details of child development	Make sure your children are getting a good education. Consult with a child development expert. Go to counseling.
Acting-out behavior of children	Make sure your children are getting a good education. Go to counseling. Spend extra "quality time" with children. Join a support group for parents. Avoid constant criticism and judgment. Avoid nagging.
Having personal space	Creatively set up private space in the home for each family member. Schedule time for personal retreat.

	Use headphones so everyone can listen to their own music.
Sharing: VCR, TV, phone, and so on	Hold family meetings to make decisions so everyone gets their fair share.
Relationships that are judgmental or argumentative	Go to counseling.
Possible genetic diseases	Consult with healthcare professionals.
All the horrific things that can happen to children	Do the best you can. Take good care of yourself. Get support from family members, friends, and others when you need it. Try counseling or peer counseling.

If you have worries related to your children, use the following space to write your worries, possible solutions, and a plan of action. Use ideas in this section, from other chapters of the book, and other solutions you have discovered.

Worry: _____

Possible solution: _____

_____

When are you going to take this action?

_____

How are going to do it?

_____

_____

_____

Worry: _____

Possible solution: _____

_____

When are you going to take this action?

_____

How are going to do it?

_____

_____

_____

Worry: _____

Possible solution: _____

_____

When are you going to take this action?

_____

How are going to do it?

_____

_____

_____

Your Family of Origin

The bond developed with your family of origin when you were young can keep you strongly attached throughout your life, even though you may be separated from them by thousands of miles or haven't seen them, or even connected with them, in many years. When there is any kind of difficulty or tragedy, the miles, years, neglect, and even estrangements often melt away and the pain is shared.

Study participants had the following worries about their families of origin:

At present there is only one really worrisome relationship in my life: my sister who lives close by. I try to be positive that eventually we will accept each other again, but part of me feels hopeless about that. I don't know what I wish except just to trust that however it works out is how it needs to work out. To do that, I just need to let go.

My relationship with my family of origin can be bothersome and can cause a lot of worry at times. That's where Alanon comes in strong.

My parents are getting older. Since they live on the other side of the continent, I see them only once a year. Each time I see them again, I become more aware of how they are aging and how their lives are becoming more and more limited. I worry about what will happen to them if one of them were to die or become incapacitated. Do they have provisions for nursing home or intensive care? Should I ask them to move closer to me? Should I try to find a place for them near us? Right now I am just biding my time, hoping against hope that they will be totally independent for many more years.

Consider the following worries related to family-of-origin members and possible solutions:

Issues That Cause Worry	Possible Solutions
Their health and safety	Take any action appropriate for you to take and then let go. Go to counseling. Attend support groups.
Who will take care of parents?	Do advance planning with them (see chapter 6, "Reducing the Possibility of Worry"). Realistically assess your own ability to care for them and do personal advance planning in case this need arises.
Wondering if you are doing as well as siblings or if family is disappointed in you	Learn to accept yourself. Go to counseling. Try peer counseling.
Wondering if family will be there for you if you are having a hard time	Realistically assess the situation. Have open, loving communication. Be there for them when possible.
Wondering why don't you have more contact, why you don't see each other more	Call and visit more often if possible (set definite times on a regular basis)
Wondering if should you spend time with them even if you don't want to	Go to counseling. Realistically assess the situation.

If you have worries that you wish to control or relieve about your family of origin, use the following space to write your worries, possible solutions, and a plan of action. Use ideas in this section, from other chapters of the book, and other solutions you have discovered.

Worry: _____

Possible solution: _____

_____

When are you going to take this action?

_____

How are going to do it?

_____

_____

_____

Worry: _____

Possible solution: _____

_____

When are you going to take this action?

_____

How are going to do it?

_____

_____

_____

Worry: _____

Possible solution: _____

_____

When are you going to take this action?

_____

How are going to do it?

_____

_____

_____

Friends and Acquaintances

Friends and acquaintances greatly contribute to the richness, security, and enjoyment of life. People in the study have varying degrees of connection to and reliance on friendships, but everyone is influenced by friends, or the lack thereof. Most people tend to worry about friends less than they worry about family members and primary partners. Of course, you generally choose your friends, thus eliminating some of the possibility of trying to relate to someone you don't have much connection with, as sometimes happens with family members. This is one reason that you may be in conflict with friends less often. People also usually do not live with friends and therefore have fewer practical issues to work out. But the importance of friendship in people's lives suggests that when worries arise, they are likely to affect you strongly. Here's what study participants had to say:

> I don't worry much about relationships, but I do work at maintaining them. I used to obsess over relationships, but have gradually learned to not be too dependent on any one relationship.

> Usually, if I stop being judgmental, I also stop worrying about what judgments the other person may have about me.

> Beginning in adolescence, I was concerned about saying or doing something that I didn't know I had done. I developed a much clearer picture of myself over the years through self-reflection and asking for feedback from others.

> Sometimes particular worries become acute. If possible I try to look as honestly as possible into myself to find out why I am so troubled about it, and try to talk it out with the person directly if I can.

> I try to respect others and communicate well. It helps some. I usually imagine problems.

> I constantly work on my relationship skills. It's been very helpful but it seems there's always room for growth in this area. I wish I could make everyone else work at it too. I can't make that happen; it's up to them.

> I worry about my friends' health. I have been spending a lot of time worrying about the health of several friends, all of whom have had suicidal periods or serious illness in the past few months. I know that all I can do is provide support, but they are on my mind a lot.

The following worries about relationships with friends were shared by study participants:

Issues That Cause Worry	Possible Solutions
Not having any friends	Join a support group.
	Attend special interest groups.
	Take educational courses.
	Volunteer for a worthy cause.
	Arrange get-togethers with acquaintances.
	Be there for others as much as they are there for you.
Whether or not people really like you	Learn to accept yourself.
	Realistically assess cues.
	Avoid imposing yourself on others.
	Avoid being too dependent, needy, loud, negative, argumentative, confrontational, or defensive.
	Take good care of your personal hygiene.
	Avoid asking too much of someone.
	Intend to give to the relationship.
	Avoid judging, criticizing, or giving too much advice.
Whether or not friends are talking about you behind your back	Work on having a sense of self-assurance.
	Stay closely connected to warm, loving, affirming people.
Whether or not you impose too much on friends	Be there for them as much as they are there for you.

If you have worries about your relationships with friends and acquaintances that you wish to control or relieve, use the following space to write your worries, possible solutions, and a plan of action. Use ideas in this section, from other chapters of the book, and other solutions you have discovered.

Worry: _____

Possible solution: _____

_____

When are you going to take this action?

_____

How are going to do it?

_____

_____

_____

Worry: _____

Possible solution: _____

_____

When are you going to take this action?

_____

How are going to do it?

_____

_____

_____

Worry: _____

Possible solution: _____

_____

When are you going to take this action?

_____

How are going to do it?

_____

_____

_____

15

Personal Issues

*I have worries because I have certain ways I
think I should be and act based on my standards.
Sometimes I'm reminded by my worries that my
standards need to be changed, or at least evaluated.*

As my friend Martha says, "Daily we create our lives." Of course we build
on past experience, our own and others', but in this society so much is new.
New roles, opportunities, and demands can be both exciting and frightening. We learn to improvise and to use our skills in new ways. We worry
about personal issues that, in a more traditional culture, were not
worrisome.

In previous chapters I addressed worries that are somewhat universal,
although how much each person worries about finances, health, or global
issues varies greatly. But there is a whole realm of worries that may spring
from circumstances, either chosen or given. A heavy person, for example,
may not relate to the worries of an underweight person. These personal
issues are some of the small and big things that define us as individuals and
may have particular worries attached to them. This chapter will not only
address worries about emotional and physical personal issues, including
gender, sexual orientation, cultural or ethnic background, religion or spiritu-
ality, weight and appearance, and living space, but will also touch on how
these issues can affect worry.

Emotional and Psychological Issues

Gender

Gender-related issues contribute significantly to your worries. Expectations placed on you because of your gender, or judgments made about you, can certainly be a cause for concern.

One woman said, "I'm pretty straightforward, but I will admit, my behavior changes when I am in mixed-gender company," while another said, "I try to remember I have power to make changes in my life, that I can take care of myself and I do not need a man to do that."

Because of your gender you may find yourself in roles you are not content with. For example, women who found themselves in caretaking roles at various times throughout their lives worried about how they could change that scenario.

> I am a mom and have been the caretaker in both my families—and I have a "caretaker" job. Probably all somewhat due to being female *and* to being the oldest child.

Statements from people in the survey certainly suggested that gender affects what people worry about.

> My husband worries about money. I worry about the children and their relationships. I worry if people love me. I work a lot on relationships—on making people like me, on being pleasant and staying connected.

> Women are socialized to worry. Also, we often feel powerless to do anything about the objects of our worry. We tend to worry about our effects on others—are we doing things right?

The following issues related to gender and gender difference that cause worry and possible solutions were shared by study participants:

Issues That Cause Worry for Women	Possible Solutions
Feeling trapped in a caretaker role	Set clear boundaries. Make yourself your highest priority. Go to counseling. Join a women's support group. Exchange ideas with women friends. Discuss with family (or whomever you are in this role with). Assess your own needs.

Sexual harassment in the workplace	Confront the perpetrator. Report the incident to a supervisor and insist on change. Contact a lawyer for advice. Check out available resources in your state. Discuss with a supportive friend.
Lower paying jobs	Insist on equal wages for equal responsibility. Seek union support.
Limited career options	Review, plan, discuss, and take action. Consult a vocational counselor. Get more education.
Self-esteem issues	Go to counseling. Write in a journal. Try peer counseling. Take time out for yourself. Use affirmations to reinforce positive self-statements. Set reasonable goals for yourself. Spend time with affirming people.
Societal expectations of how you should look and act	Confront and let go of your own stereotypes. Be active in an advocacy group. Build your self-esteem. Be clear about who you are and how you want to look. Find role models appropriate for your life stage.
Lack of power	Join a women's group. Volunteer for a women's organization. Position yourself in places of power. Learn to speak clearly and with confidence. Take a leadership role in your department or in an organization. Spend time with positive mentors.
Unequal treatment	Challenge inequities. Work for a women's organization. Advocate for disenfranchised women.

Issues That Cause Worry for Men	Possible Solutions
Lack of intimacy	Build a strong support system of others with mutual interests and values.
	Talk openly with others to help them feel free to open up.
	Join or start a support group.
Feeling emotionally repressed	Try counseling or peer counseling.
	Read about how other men have worked with this problem.
	Join a support group.
Societal expectations	Act according to your personal beliefs.
	Be clear about what your beliefs are.
Self-esteem issues	Join a support group.
	Go to counseling.
	Write in a journal.
	Try peer counseling.
	Take time out for yourself.
	Use affirmations to reinforce positive self-statements.
	Spend time with affirming people.
	Set reasonable goals for yourself.
Providing family financial support	See chapter 12, "Financial Worries."

If you have worries about issues relating to your gender that you wish to control or relieve, use the following space to write your worries, possible solutions, and a plan of action. Use ideas in this section, from other chapters of the book, and other solutions you have discovered.

Worry: _____

Possible solution: _____

_____

When are you going to take this action?

_____

How are you going to do it?

_____

_____

_____

Worry: _____

Possible solution: _____

_____

When are you going to take this action?

_____

How are you going to do it?

_____

_____

_____

Worry: _____

Possible solution: _____

_____

When are you going to take this action?

_____

How are you going to do it?

_____

_____

_____

Sexual Orientation

In compiling the findings of the study, I discovered that people who are gay, lesbian, or bisexual experience some worries that are quite different from people who are heterosexual.

> I know that most women worry about their safety. But I think being a lesbian woman makes me an even more attractive target. I limit where I go, trying to avoid potentially dangerous situations.

Worrying about getting AIDS is of course more prevalent in the gay community than in the general population. Being part of a high-risk group for a potentially devastating and deadly illness is worrisome, to say the least. One man reports that being in a monogamous relationship for the last ten years has relieved this worry. Before that, prior to anonymous testing, he lived for several years with the worry that he had AIDS. He dealt with that worry by keeping his life as rich and full as possible. Today, the use of preventive measures, which include using condoms, preventing the exchange of body fluids, and restricting sexual contact, is helping to control this worry for many people.

Added to the worry of contracting AIDS is the worry about the illness and painful death of close friends. A young gay man said:

> I have lost my best friend and several close friends and neighbors. At one point, I attended three funerals in two months. At times I feel alone and disconnected from my past. I worry about this less since the new drugs seem to prolong the health and lives of friends with HIV. I worry about losing those people who are left. In fact a sister I was very close to and an ex-lover have also died (non-AIDS related). I try to appreciate and stay close to those friends and family members I have.

Stereotyping, prejudice, and hate crimes are other issues that cause worry for people who are not heterosexual. An older man shared the following incident:

> I had just left a restaurant with my partner, my sister, and her friend. A car stopped as if to ask for directions. My partner walked over to the car and was sprayed with a fire extinguisher. It felt terrible. I also have been treated as if I am inferior because I am gay, particularly in work situations. My ability to do my work and do it well have carried me through.

A gay man in his thirties had worries related to his family's rejection of him. He used to have a hard time with being gay and what it symbolized, but he said,

> I have dealt with and let go of my father's rejection by accepting the fact that I don't fit into his framework and that he believes I'm a sinner because I'm gay.

Having been part of the gay community for many years, one man feels that the experience of being gay and being accepted in this country has changed radically over the last twenty-five years. Now at age fifty-seven, he feels that society has a different perception of sexual orientation issues. As a young man, he had a bad experience with "coming out" that taught him to be more "cagey" about being gay: he told a friend with whom he had grown up that he was gay, and she never spoke to him again. He says he has never, in all his fifty-seven years, told his mother he's gay.

The following issues that cause worries and possible solutions related to sexual orientation were shared by study participants:

Issues That Cause Worries	Possible Solutions
Being the victim of hate crimes	Join a support group. Take self-defense classes. Be cautious in dangerous situations. Report hate crimes so others are not victimized.
Not having children	Realize you could play an important role in the lives of nieces and nephews and friends' children. Find out about artificial insemination or adoption.
Standing out, being different	Practice self-acceptance. Join a support group. Develop a circle of close friends. Spend time with others with the same sexual orientation.
Lack of family support	Build close connections with people who are supportive. Set up a new family, choosing friends to take the place of family members who are not supportive. Go to counseling.
Loneliness	Join a support group. Attend community events. Arrange outings with acquaintances. Be there for others as much as they are there for you. Go to counseling.
Loss of children through court action	Seek legal help.
Alienation of children through hostility of former spouse	Engage in family mediation.
Ostracism of children by peers	Participate in school events. Pretend to be straight on public occasions (this may understandably be unacceptable to some people). Create a welcoming home for your children's friends.

If you have worries about issues relating to your sexual orientation that you wish to control or relieve, use the following space to write your worries, possible solutions, and a plan of action. Use ideas in this section, from other chapters of the book, and other solutions you have discovered.

Worry: _____

Possible solution: _____

_____

When are you going to take this action?

_____

How are you going to do it?

_____

_____

_____

Worry: _____

Possible solution: _____

_____

When are you going to take this action?

_____

How are you going to do it?

_____

_____

_____

Worry: _____

Possible solution: _____

_____

When are you going to take this action?

_____

How are you going to do it?

_____

_____

_____

Religious, Cultural, or Ethnic Background

Some people felt that their religion, culture, and ethnicity have been a great asset in their lives, while others felt these things caused them considerable worry and pain. Consider the following statements from study participants:

Unfortunately, my early upbringing affected me negatively. I was encouraged to worry and to behave out of fear. Some of those memories still come up unexpectedly. "Hell" is a good worry topic, for instance. I don't really believe in hell—unless it is misery in this life—but something in me still worries about torment after death. I believe in using my powers of observation, reason, intuition, and caring. But some worry is irrational and can't be touched by reason.

Born and raised in a small community, worrying was part of the culture. I learned to worry from all the other women in the community. I didn't realize I didn't have to worry about every little thing until friends started pointing that out to me when I went away to college.

Being a Mormon has caused me a lot of worry. It is so rigid it makes you kind of want to be perfect, and you can't be perfect.

Jewish people often worry a lot. I blame it on history. Anti-Jewish attitudes are widespread. I try to keep things in perspective. I don't deny or emphasize my Jewish heritage.

Catholicism taught me fear, which is, I think, a basis of worry. I try to counteract this by educating myself through conversation, reading, and so on.

Catholic guilt is very powerful. So is Irish guilt. I am a recovering Catholic. I talk to other people with similar backgrounds.

I came from a cultural background where worry was the norm, especially for the women in the family. I think we worried because if we didn't, things wouldn't turn out okay. It was a part of dealing with life.

I am a Wiccan—pagan. I worry about people believing that my beliefs are evil or crazy. I worry about how to openly live according to my spiritual beliefs without being judged or putting down anyone else's beliefs. I study religion in general and try to focus on the parallels between my beliefs and other beliefs.

I just consider myself to have spiritual beliefs. In general, this aspect of life helps me to worry much less and about fewer things. Sometimes I worry about being hypocritical. I try to practice and live what I teach others. This always continues to result in a deepening of my spiritual basis in life and therefore even less worry occurs.

My parents both experienced the Depression full force. They instilled in me a strong work/worry ethic. If you've got a purgative for it, I'd sure like to order some! I go to yard sales, sew my own clothes, cook from scratch, only see shows at the $1 theater, and a myriad of nonsense my parents also do, although they are wealthy now.

Study participants shared the following issues related to their religious, cultural, or ethnic background that caused worry and possible solutions:

Issues That Cause Worry	Possible Solutions
Guilt, sin, shame about everything	Go to counseling. Work on changing negative thoughts to positive ones (see chapter 3, "Techniques for Dealing with Worry"). Work on self-acceptance, forgiveness, and letting go. Study and read from progressive theologians. Seek pastoral counseling from an accredited source. Learn about your ancestry. Find a supportive peer group.
Loss of heritage, cultural, or religious connections	Study your heritage, culture, or religion. Preserve the culture or religion in your family. Plan holidays or other events that emphasize tradition.
Alienation from family of origin	Maintain contact. Remember special days or events. Validate your family's cultural experiences.
Standing out, being different	Practice self-acceptance. Focus on shared qualities.

If you have worries about issues related to your cultural or ethnic background that you wish to control or relieve, use the following space to write your worries, possible solutions, and a plan of action. Use ideas in this section, from other chapters of the book, and other solutions you have discovered.

Worry: _____

Possible solution: _____

_____

When are you going to take this action?

_____

How are you going to do it?

_____

_____

_____

Worry: _____

Possible solution: _____

_____

When are you going to take this action?

_____

How are you going to do it?

_____

_____

_____

Worry: _____

Possible solution: _____

_____

When are you going to take this action?

_____

How are you going to do it?

_____

_____

_____

Physical Issues

Appearance

Most people worry about some aspect of their appearance. Especially in this media-driven society, it's hard not to. Others have worried in the past but have reached a realistic place of self-acceptance.

Here are some of the thoughts from study participants on worries about appearance:

> I go through phases of concern, but generally, I'm casual and comfortable. If people don't like my looks, I figure they can look a different direction.

> If I feel I look attractive, my self-confidence is bolstered. I try to be well groomed all the time.

> I hate worrying about appearance, but sometimes I do. I try to look as good as I can, and sometimes, often, I just tell myself that it's not very important.

> Again, I'd like to have enough confidence not to care about appearance. Our culture makes it difficult.

> I had severe acne when I was younger. It was a drag. It's much better now, but I still worry about scarring.

> I do have an interesting nose that on a few occasions has been commented about. I learned early to accept my nose as a part of me and not to worry. Recently, I've been noticing other people with similar noses!

More people worry about weight, usually weight gain or being overweight, than about any other aspect of their appearance:

> I used to worry constantly about my weight, which has been way out of control since I was a kid. I would obsess about weight and appearance to the point of feeling totally worthless and being too ashamed to go anywhere. It has taken a lot of therapy to even begin to deal with this problem. I work at reminding myself that it's not worth wasting my life because I don't fit society's view of beauty. I spend my time with people who are concerned with the person on the inside.

The following appearance issues that cause worry and possible solutions were shared by study participants:

Issues That Cause Worry	Possible Solutions
Being overweight	Practice self-acceptance.
	Focus on how you look and feel rather than how much you weigh and take action accordingly—for example, buy yourself an attractive outfit.
	Experiment with popular diets and find out what works for you.
	Keep a food journal.
	Make exercise a high priority.
	Change your eating habits—avoid sugar, fried and fatty foods, and junk foods.
	Focus your diet on healthy, natural foods.
	Keep junk foods and foods you are trying to avoid out of your house.
	Eat smaller meals more often.
	Think before you eat.
	Refer to chapter 13, "Health Issues."
	Drink plenty of water.
	Eat only when sitting down at a table.
	Plan to lose weight slowly—one to two pounds a week maximum.
	Set small goals and reward yourself when you reach them.
	Develop a personal weight loss plan that works for you.
	Consult a nutritionist.
	Join a support group for people who are trying to lose weight.
Being too skinny	Drink protein-fortified shakes.
	See a nutritionist.
	Keep foods on hand that are healthy and that you enjoy eating.
	Eat regular meals; avoiding skipping meals.
Fitting in	Practice self-acceptance.
	Dress in whatever feels right to you and then forget about it.
Being in style	Peruse fashion magazines.
	Be aware of what others are wearing.

Issues That Cause Worry	Possible Solutions
Disproportionate body parts	Practice self-acceptance. Avoid comparing yourself with others. Celebrate diversity.
Wrinkles	Use Retina-A. Use sunblocking and moisturizers. Avoid smoking and secondhand smoke.
Looking old	Accept yourself as an attractive, mature person. Find a flattering, simple hair style and stick with it. Wear fashionable but not extreme styles.

I have worries related to my appearance.

_____ Yes

_____ No

If so, what are they?

Worry: _____

Possible solution: _____

_____

When are you going to take this action?

_____

How are you going to do it?

_____

_____

_____

Worry: _____

Possible solution: _____

_____

When are you going to take this action?

_____

How are you going to do it?

_____

_____

_____

Worry: _____

Possible solution: _____

_____

When are you going to take this action?

_____

How are you going to do it?

_____

_____

_____

Epilogue

This book is not one to be read once and then forgotten. I hope you will use parts of it now, then pick it up again in a few weeks or months. As your life moves along, ideas that didn't seem interesting before may suddenly seem to be an answer.

The following prose is from a friend of many years.

Today

I worried about whether to charge $7.00 or $8.00 for house-sitting next week.

Also I worried about what will be happening tomorrow while I'm busy doing something else.

My boss has set up a "little meeting" on Friday with me. Oh, dear—worry Big Time.

And what about that ice cream bar I ate last week? Where did it settle and how much did my blood pressure go up because of it? Arrrrgh!

Now I'm worrying about how *all this* worrying is affecting my blood pressure.

Ongoing worries are . . . why do I have an endless supply of very large flies in my apartment? . . .

Will the 3rd Street Curiosity Shoppe buy the twin bed I have for sale for $25.00

. . . Who's gonna miss me when I'm gone?

Yours in the true spirit of worry . . .

Mary Liz Riddle

Resources

Publications, Phone Numbers, and Software Programs That Can Help Control Worry

Addictions

Catalano, E., and N. Sonenberg. 1993. *Consuming Passions: Help for Compulsive Shoppers*. Oakland, Calif.: New Harbinger Publications.

Center for Substance Abuse and Mental Health Services Administration (SAMHSA). 1997. *National Clearinghouse for Alcohol and Drug Information Publications Catalog*. Washington, D.C.: SAMSHA.

Estes, K., and M. Siegal. 1992. *Behind the 8-Ball: A Guide for Families of Gamblers*. New York: Simon & Schuster.

Fanning, P., and J. O'Neill. 1996. *The Addiction Workbook: A Step-by-Step Guide To Quitting Alcohol & Drugs*. Oakland, Calif.: New Harbinger Publications.

Gamblers Anonymous. 1984. *Sharing Recovery Through Gamblers Anonymous*. Los Angeles: Gamblers Anonymous.

Johnson, V. 1980. *I'll Quit Tomorrow*. New York: Harper and Row.

Roselline, G., and M. Worden. 1997. *Of Course You're Angry: A Guide to Dealing with the Emotions of Substance Abuse*. Center City, Minn.: Hazelden.

Roth, G. 1993. *Breaking Free from Compulsive Eating*. New York: NAL-Dutton.

———. 1992. *When Food Is Love: Exploring the Relationship Between Eating & Intimacy.* New York: NAL-Dutton.

Stevic-Rust, L., and A. Maximin. 1996. *The Stop Smoking Workbook: Your Guide to Healthy Quitting.* Oakland, Calif.: New Harbinger Publications.

AIDS

CDC National AIDS Information & Referral Hotline: (800) 342-AIDS.

Kübler-Ross, E. 1987. *AIDS: The Ultimate Challenge.* New York: Macmillan.

National AIDS Clearinghouse (educational resources): (800) 458-5231.

The People with AIDS Coalition: (800) 828-3280.

PROJECT INFORM (treatment and therapies): (800) 822-7422.

Alzheimer's Disease

Contact your local Council on Aging or call the information line for your state for local resources.

Alzheimer's Association (National Information Line): (800) 621-0379.

Dippel, R., and J. Hutton. 1988. *Caring for the Alzheimer's Patient: A Practical Guide.* Buffalo, N.Y.: Prometheus Books.

Mace, N., and P. Rabins. 1991. *36-Hour Day: A Family Guide to Caring for Persons with Alzheimer's Disease, Related Dementing Illnesses, and Memory Loss in Later Life.* Baltimore: Johns Hopkins University Press.

Aromatherapy

Fischer-Rizzi, S. 1990. *Complete Aromatherapy.* New York: Sterling Publishing Co.

Worwood, V. 1991. *The Complete Book of Essential Oils & Aromatherapy.* Novato, Calif.: New World Library.

Breath Work

Ramacharaka, Y. 1996. *Science of Breath.* Eliot, Maine: Taraporevala Sons & Co.

Sky, M. 1990. *Breathing: Expanding Your Power & Energy.* Santa Fe, N. Mex.: Bear & Company Publishing, 1990.

Career and Work Issues

Bolles, R. 1997. *The 1998 What Color Is Your Parachute?* Berkeley, Calif.: Ten Speed Press.

Freudenberger, H., and G. North. 1985. *Women's Burnout: How to Spot It, How to Reverse It, and How to Prevent It.* New York: Penguin Books.

Hakim, C. 1994. *We Are All Self-Employed: The New Social Contract for Working in a Changed World.* San Francisco: Berrett-Koehler Publishers.

Irish, R. 1987. *Go Hire Yourself an Employer*. New York: Doubleday.

O'Hara, V. 1995. *Wellness at Work: Building Resilience to Job Stress*. Oakland, Calif.: New Harbinger Publications.

Pines, A., and E. Aronson. 1988. *Career Burnout: Causes and Cures*. New York: Free Press.

Tieger, P., and B. Barron-Tieger. 1995. *Do What You Are: Discover the Perfect Career for You Through the Secrets of Personality Type*. New York: Little, Brown & Co.

Weiss, R. 1990. *Staying the Course: The Emotional and Social Lives of Men Who Do Well at Work*. New York: Free Press.

Changing Negative Thoughts to Positive Ones

Burns, D. 1990. *The Feeling Good Handbook*. New York: Plume.

————. 1980. *Feeling Good*. New York: Morrow.

Copeland, M. E. 1992. *The Depression Workbook: A Guide to Living with Depression and Manic Depression*. Oakland, Calif.: New Harbinger Publications.

Fanning, P., and M. McKay. 1991. *Prisoners of Belief*. Oakland, Calif.: New Harbinger Publications.

McKay, M., M. Davis, and P. Fanning. 1997. *Thoughts and Feelings: Taking Control of Your Moods and Your Life*, second edition. Oakland, Calif.: New Harbinger Publications.

Dealing with Children

Frain, B., and E. Clegg. 1997. *Becoming a Wise Parent for Your Grown Child: How to Give Love and Support without Meddling*. Oakland, Calif.: New Harbinger Publications.

Gordon, T. 1990. *P.E.T.: Parent Effectiveness Training*. New York: New American Library.

Newman, M. 1994. *Stepfamily Realities: How to Overcome Difficulties and Have a Happy Family*. Oakland, Calif.: New Harbinger Publications.

Paleg, K. 1997. *The Ten Things Every Parent Needs to Know: A Guide for New Parents and Everyone Else Who Cares about Children*. Oakland, Calif.: New Harbinger Publications.

Pantley, E. 1996. *Kid Cooperation: How to Stop Yelling, Nagging, and Pleading and Get Kids to Cooperate*. Oakland, Calif.: New Harbinger Publications.

Dealing with Parents

Becker, M. 1993. *Last Touch: Preparing for a Parent's Death*. Oakland, Calif.: New Harbinger Publications.

Bloomfield, H., with L. Felder. 1983. *Making Peace with Your Parents*. New York: Random House.

Levin, N. 1997. *How to Care for Your Parents: A Practical Guide to Eldercare.* New York: W. W. Norton & Co.

Death of a Loved One

Caplan, S., and G. Lang. 1995. *Grief's Courageous Journey: A Workbook.* Oakland, Calif.: New Harbinger Publications.

Doka, K. 1996. *Living with Grief after Sudden Loss: Suicide, Homicide, Accident, Heart Attack, Stroke.* Bristol, Penn.: Taylor & Francis.

Karnes, B. 1991. *My Friend, I Care: The Grief Experience.* (Contact Barbara Karnes, RN., P.O. Box 335, Stilwell, KS 66085.)

————. 1986. *Gone from My Sight: The Dying Experience.* (Contact Barbara Karnes, RN., P.O. Box 335, Stilwell, KS 6608.5)

Kübler-Ross, E. 1969. *On Death and Dying.* New York: Macmillan.

Nadeau, J. 1997. *Families Making Sense of Death.* Thousand Oaks, Calif.: Sage Publications.

Staudacher, C. 1987. *Beyond Grief: A Guide for Recovering from the Death of a Loved One.* Oakland, Calif.: New Harbinger Publications.

Financial Concerns

Abentrod, S. 1996. *10 Minute Guide to Beating Debt.* New York: Macmillan.

Case, S. 1997. *The First Book of Investing: The Absolute Beginners Guide to Building Wealth Safely.* Rocklin, Calif.: Prima Publishers.

Dominguez, J., and V. Robin 1992. *Your Money or Your Life: Transforming Your Relationship with Money and Achieving Financial Independence.* New York: Penguin Books.

Hunt, M. 1997. *The Complete Cheapskate: How to Break Free From the Money Worries Forever, without Sacrificing the Quality of Your Life.* Colorado Springs, Colo.: Focus on the Family Publishers.

————. 1995. *The Cheapskate Monthly Money Makeover.* New York: St. Martin's Press.

Lawrence, J. 1997. *The Budget Kit: The Common Cents Money Management Workbook.* Chicago: Dearborn Trade.

Loungo, T. 1997. *10 Minute Guide to Household Budgeting.* Indianapolis, Ind.: Macmillan General Reference.

McCullough, B. 1996. *Bonnie's Household Budget Book: The Essential Workbook for Getting Control of Your Money.* New York: St. Martin's Press.

Naylor, W. 1997. *10 Steps to Financial Success: A Beginners Guide to Saving and Investing.* New York: John Wiley & Son.

Orman, S. 1997. *The 9 Steps to Financial Freedom.* New York: Crown Publishers.

Pond, J. 1997. *4 Easy Steps to Successful Investing.* New York: Avon Books.

————. 1992. *1001 Ways to Cut Your Expenses.* New York: Dell Books.

Software: Quicken Deluxe 98; Quicken Home and Business 98; Managing Your Money 2.0; Money 98; The Stock Shop with Peter Lynch; Window on Wall Street: Deluxe Investor; VersaCheck.

Focusing

Copeland, M. E. 1994. *Living Without Depression and Manic Depression.* Oakland, Calif.: New Harbinger Publications.

Cornell, A. 1996. *The Power of Focusing.* Oakland, Calif.: New Harbinger Publications.

Gendlin, E. 1981. *Focusing.* New York: Bantam Books.

Guided Visualization

M. Davis, E. Eshelman, and M. McKay. 1997. *Relaxation & Stress Reduction Workbook.* Oakland, Calif.: New Harbinger Publications.

Fanning, P. 1994. *Visualization for Change.* Oakland, Calif.: New Harbinger Publications.

McKay, M., M. Davis, and P. Fanning. 1997. *Thoughts and Feelings: Taking Control of Your Moods and Your Life,* second edition. Oakland, Calif.: New Harbinger Publications.

Samuels, M., and N. Samuels. 1975. *Seeing with the Mind's Eye: The History, Techniques, and Uses of Visualization.* New York: Random House.

Health-Related Issues

Balch, J., and P. Balch. 1997. *Prescription for Nutritional Healing.* New York: Avery Publishing Group.

Barnes, B., and L. Galton. 1976. *Hypothyroidism: The Unsuspected Illness.* New York: HarperCollins Publishers.

Benson, H., and E. Stuart. 1992. *The Wellness Book: The Comprehensive Guide to Maintaining Health and Treating Stress-Related Illness.* New York: Simon & Schuster.

Cash, T. 1997. *The Body Image Workbook: An 8-Step Program for Learning to Like Your Looks.* Oakland, Calif.: New Harbinger Publications.

Catalano, E., and K. Hardin. 1996. *The Chronic Pain Control Workbook,* second edition. Oakland, Calif.: New Harbinger Publications.

Consumer Guide Editors. 1995. *Prescription Drugs.* New York: NAL-Dutton.

Crook, W. 1986. *The Yeast Connection: A Medical Breakthrough.* New York: Vintage.

Ferguson, J. 1988. *Habits, Not Diets: The Secret to Lifetime Weight Control.* Palo Alto, Calif.: Bull Publishing Co.

Goldberg, B. 1993. *Alternative Medicine Guide to Chronic Fatigue, Fibromyalgia, and Environmental Illness.* Tiburon, Calif.: Future Medicine Publishers.

Langer, S. 1995. *Solved: The Riddle of Illness.* New Canaan, Conn.: Keats Publishing.

Ostrom, N. 1993. *Fifty Things You Should Know about Chronic Fatigue Syndrome.* New York: St. Martin's Press.

Rector-Page, L. 1996. *Healthy Healing: A Guide to Self-Healing for Everyone.* Sonora, Calif.: Healthy Healing Publications.

Rosenthal, N. 1993. *Winter Blues.* New York: Guilford Press.

Sears, B., and W. Lawren. 1995. *The Zone: A Dietary Road Map.* New York: HarperCollins Publishers.

Homeopathy

Cummings, S., and D. Ullman. 1984. *Everybody's Guide to Homeopathic Medicines: Taking Care of Yourself and Your Family with Safe and Effective Remedies.* New York: G. P. Putnam's Sons.

Ullman, D. 1995. *The Consumer's Guide to Homeopathy: The Definitive Resource for Understanding Homeopathic Medicine and Making It Work for You.* New York: G. P. Putnam's Sons.

Men's Issues

Fanning, P., and M. McKay 1993. *Being A Man: A Guide to the New Masculinity.* Oakland, Calif.: New Harbinger Publications.

Johnson, B. 1997. *Coming Out Every Day: A Gay, Bisexual, or Questioning Man's Guide.* Oakland, Calif.: New Harbinger Publications.

Real, T. 1997. *I Don't Want to Talk about It: Overcoming the Secret Legacy of Male Depression.* New York: Simon & Schuster.

Staudacher, C. 1992. *Men & Grief.* Oakland, Calif.: New Harbinger Publications.

Mental Health Issues

Birkedahl, N. 1990. *The Habit Control Workbook.* Oakland, Calif.: New Harbinger Publications.

Borysenko, J. 1990. *Guilt Is the Teacher, Love Is the Lesson.* New York: Warner Books.

Bourne, E. 1995. *The Anxiety & Phobia Workbook,* second edition. Oakland, Calif.: New Harbinger Publications.

Copeland, M. E. 1997. *WRAP: Wellness Recovery Action Plan.* Brattleboro, Vt: Peach Press. (To order, call [802] 254-2092)

———. 1994. *Living Without Depression and Manic Depression: A Workbook for Maintaining Mood Stability.* Oakland, Calif.: New Harbinger Publications.

———. 1992. *The Depression Workbook: A Guide for Living with Depression and Manic Depression.* Oakland, Calif.: New Harbinger Publications.

Finney, L. 1996. *Clear Your Past, Change Your Future: Proven Techniques for Inner Exploration and Healing.* Oakland, Calif.: New Harbinger Publications.

Forward, S. 1989. *Toxic Parents: Overcoming Their Hurtful Legacy and Reclaiming Your Life.* New York: Bantam Books.

Kabat-Zinn, J. 1990. *Full Catastrophe Living.* New York: Delacorte Press.

Markway, B., C. Carmin, C. Pollard, and T. Flynn. 1992. *Dying of Embarrassment: Help for Social Anxiety and Social Phobia.* Oakland, Calif.: New Harbinger Publications.

McKay, M., and P. Fanning. 1987. *Self Esteem,* second edition. Oakland, Calif.: New Harbinger Publications.

McKinley, R. 1989. *Personal Peace: Transcending Your Interpersonal Limits.* Oakland, Calif.: New Harbinger Publications.

Starlanyl, D., and M. Copeland. 1996. *Fibromyalgia and Chronic Myofascial Pain Syndrome: A Survival Manual.* Oakland, Calif.: New Harbinger Publications.

Steketee, G., and K. White. 1990. *When Once Is Not Enough: Help for Obsessive Compulsives.* Oakland, Calif.: New Harbinger Publications.

Walsch, N. D. 1996. *Conversations with God: An Uncommon Dialogue, Book 1.* New York: G. P. Putnam's Sons.

White, B., and E. Madera, eds. 1997. *The Self-Help Source Book: Finding & Forming Mutual Aid Self-Help Groups.* Denville, N.J.: American Self-Help Clearinghouse, Northwest Covenant Medical Center. (To order, call [201] 625-7101)

Wolpe, J. 1988. *Life Without Fear: Anxiety and Its Cure.* Oakland, Calif.: New Harbinger Publications.

Zuercher-White, E. 1998. *An End To Panic: Breakthrough Techniques for Overcoming Panic Disorder,* second edition. Oakland, Calif.: New Harbinger Publications.

Organization

Aslett, D. 1984. *Clutter's Last Stand.* Cincinnati, Ohio: Reader's Digest Books.

Software: ACT!; Day-Timer Organizer 98; Ecco Pro; Lotus Organizer 97 GS; Project Manager Pro; Small Business Start-Up; Success Inc: Business Plan; Business Plan Pro.

Peer Counseling

Copeland, M. E. 1997. *WRAP: Wellness Recovery Action Plan.* Brattleboro, Vt: Peach Press. (To order, call [802] 254-2092.)

————. 1994. *Living Without Depression And Manic Depression: A Workbook for Maintaining Mood Stability.* Oakland, Calif.: New Harbinger Publications.

————. 1992. *The Depression Workbook: A Guide for Living with Depression and Manic Depression.* Oakland, Calif.: New Harbinger Publications.

Relationship Issues

Beattie, M. 1989. *Beyond Codependency.* New York: Harper & Row.

Brinegar, J. 1992. *Breaking Free from Domestic Violence.* Minneapolis, Minn: CompCare Publishers.

Enns, G., and J. Black. 1997. *It's Not Okay Anymore: Your Personal Guide to Ending Abuse, Taking Charge, and Loving Yourself.* Oakland, Calif.: New Harbinger Publications.

Evans, P. 1992. *The Verbally Abusive Relationship: How to Recognize It and How to Respond.* Holbrook, Mass.: Bob Adams, Inc.

Kingma, D. 1987. *Coming Apart: Why Relationships End and How to Live Through the Ending of Yours.* Berkeley, Calif.: Conari Press.

Lerner, H. 1985. *The Dance of Anger: A Woman's Guide to Changing the Patterns of Intimate Relationships.* New York: Harper & Row.

Heyn, D. 1997. *Marriage Shock: The Transformation of Women into Wives.* New York: Villard Books.

McKay, M., M. Davis, and P. Fanning. 1995. *Messages: The Communication Skills Book,* second edition. Oakland, Calif.: New Harbinger Publications.

McKay, M., R. Rogers, J. Blades, and R. Gosse. 1984. *The Divorce Book: A Practical and Compassionate Guide.* Oakland, Calif.: New Harbinger Publications.

Miller, A. 1990. *The Enabler: When Helping Harms the Ones You Love.* New York: Ballantine Books.

Rubin, T. 1969. *The Angry Book.* New York: Collier Books.

Savage, E. 1997. *Don't Take It Personally!: The Art of Dealing with Rejection.* Oakland, Calif.: New Harbinger Publications.

Scott, G. 1990. *Resolving Conflict: With Others and Within Yourself.* Oakland, Calif.: New Harbinger Publications.

Woodhouse, V., and V. Collins, with M. Blakeman. 1995. *Divorce & Money: How to Make the Best Financial Decisions During Divorce.* Berkeley, Calif.: Nolo Press.

Relaxation and Stress Reduction

Benson, H. and W. Proctor. 1985. *Beyond the Relaxation Response.* New York: Berkley Publishing Group.

Bricklin, M., M. Golin, D. Grandenetti, and A. Leiberman. 1990. *Positive Living and Health.* Emmaus, Penn.: Rodale Press.

Davis, M., E. Eschelman, and M. McKay. 1995. *The Relaxation & Stress Reduction Workbook.* Oakland, Calif.: New Harbinger Publications.

Flach, F. 1985. *Resilience: Discovering a New Strength in Times of Stress.* New York: Fawcett.

Hay, L. 1987. *Heal Your Life and Body.* Santa Monica, Calif.: Hay House.

McKay, M., and P. Fanning. 1997. *The Daily Relaxer.* Oakland, Calif.: New Harbinger Publications.

O'Hara, V. 1996. *Five Weeks to Healing Stress: The Wellness Option.* Oakland, Calif.: New Harbinger Publications.

Serious Illness

Deardorff, W., and J. Reeves. 1997. *Preparing for Surgery: A Mind-Body Approach to Enhance Healing and Recovery.* Oakland, Calif.: New Harbinger Publications.

Gersh, W., W. Golden, and D. Robbins. 1997. *Mind Over Malignancy: Living with Cancer.* Oakland, Calif.: New Harbinger Publications.

Karnes, B. 1994. *A Time to Live: Living with a Life-Threatening Illness.* (Contact Barbara Karnes, RN., P.O. Box 335, Stilwell, KS 66085.)

Weisman, A. 1984. *The Coping Capacity: On the Nature of Being Mortal.* New York: Human Sciences Press.

Self-Hypnosis

Alman, B., and P. Lambrou. 1992. *Self-Hypnosis: The Complete Manual For Health and Self Change.* New York: Brunner/Mazel.

Hadley, J., and C. Staudacher. 1996. *Hypnosis For Change,* second edition. Oakland, Calif.: New Harbinger Publications.

Victim of Violence

Adams, C., and J. Fay. 1989. *Free of the Shadows: Recovering from Sexual Violence.* Oakland, Calif.: New Harbinger Publications.

Goldman, L. 1996. *Breaking the Silence: A Guide to Help Children with Complicated Grief—Suicide, Homicide, AIDS, Violence and Abuse.* Washington, D.C.: Taylor & Francis.

Herman, J. 1992. *Trauma and Recovery: The Aftermath of Violence, from Domestic Abuse to Political Terror.* New York: Basic Books.

Matsakis, A. 1996. *I Can't Get Over It: A Handbook for Survivors,* second edition. Oakland, Calif.: New Harbinger Publications.

———. 1991. *When the Bough Breaks: A Helping Guide for Parents of Sexually Abused Children.* Oakland, Calif.: New Harbinger Publications.

Women's Health

Boston Women's Health Collective. 1992. *The New Our Bodies, Ourselves.* New York: Simon & Schuster.

Doress-Worters, P., and D. Siegal, in cooperation with the Boston Women's Health Collective. 1996. *The New Ourselves Growing Older: Women Aging with Knowledge and Power.* New York: Peter Smith Press.

Huston, J., and L. Lanka. 1997. *Perimenopause: Changes in Women's Health After 35.* Oakland, Calif.: New Harbinger Publications.

Love, S., with K. Lindsay. 1995. *Dr. Susan Love's Breast Book.* New York: Addison-Wesley.

Lush, J., and P. Rushford. 1987. *Emotional Phases of a Woman's Life.* Old Tappen, N.J.: Fleming H. Revell Co.

Scarf, M. 1980. *Unfinished Business: Pressure Points in the Lives of Women.* New York: Doubleday.

Toll-Free Numbers

See "Community Service Numbers" in the first section of your telephone directory.

Call the Bell Atlantic Directory Store, 1 (888) BOOKS-65, to order any of the following directories:

The Toll-Free Phone Book USA $25

AT&T National Shoppers Guide $13

International Business Buyers Guide $20

(These directories are updated frequently and their prices fluctuate with sales.)

References

American Psychological Association. 1994. *Diagnostic and Statistical Manual of Mental Disorders,* fourth edition (*DSM-IV*). Washington, D.C.: American Psychological Association.

Balch, J., and P. Balch. 1993. *Prescription for Nutritional Healing: A Practical A-Z Reference to Drug-Free Remedies Using Vitamins, Minerals, Herbs, and Food Supplements.* New York: Avery Publishing Group.

Barlow, D., and M. Craske. 1994. *Mastery of Your Anxiety and Panic II.* Albany, N.Y.: Graywind Publications.

Borkovec, T. D. 1994. The nature, functions, and origins of worry. In *Worry: Perspectives on Theory, Assessment, and Treatment,* edited by Graham Davey and Frank Tallis. West Sussex, England: John Wiley & Sons.

Davey, G. 1994. Worrying and problem-solving. In *Worry: Perspectives on Theory, Assessment, and Treatment,* edited by Graham Davey and Frank Tallis. West Sussex, England: John Wiley & Sons.

Fanning, P. 1994. *Visualization for Change,* second edition. Oakland, Calif.: New Harbinger Publications.

Hadley, J., and C. Staudacher. 1996. *Hypnosis for Change,* third edition. Oakland, Calif.: New Harbinger Publications.

Hallowell, E. M. 1997. *Worry: Controlling It and Using It Wisely.* New York: Pantheon Books.

Hoehn-Saric, R., and D. R. McLeod. 1988. The peripheral sympathetic nervous system: Its role in normal and pathologic anxiety. *Psychiatric Clinics of North America,* 11:375–386.